UNDER THE GUN

A children's hospital on the front line
of an American crisis

UNDER THE GUN

A children's hospital on the front line
of an American crisis

Stu Durando

For Riley, Bennett and Elizabethe

Table of Contents

Author's Note

Much of the research for this book was conducted through interviews with employees of St. Louis Children's Hospital and shooting victims and their family members. In keeping with the Health Insurance Portability and Accountability Act (HIPAA), patients and family members signed consent forms before they were interviewed and before personnel at the hospital could discuss their cases. Some families asked for names to be shortened or for pseudonyms to be used. In some cases, they agreed to allow their surgeries to be witnessed.

D.O.A.

Death seemed likely for 15-year-old Trevin Gamble as he lay on his back in a St. Louis alley littered with 9-millimeter shell casings. One minute he was walking with three friends. The next, a random insult directed at a passer-by was answered with gunfire. A bullet blew a hole in his chest before exiting through his back.

Paramedics rushed Trevin to St. Louis Children's Hospital, where he arrived without vital signs. Police officers who went to the hospital wrote in their report of the dire circumstances, listing the teen as "critical with death being imminent." Next of kin were notified.

Trevin arrived at 3:35 p.m. to a trauma bay operating under ideal circumstances. The hospital was heavily staffed. Surgeons were exhaling after completing the day's scheduled cases. Nurses and physicians were beginning shifts in preparation for the emergency room's busiest hours. The teaching hospital was teeming with medical students and residents, who are known to assemble in large numbers when something extraordinary is unfolding. Some would be participants, and some would be spectators. But all would learn something as immediate and extraordinary life-saving techniques would be required.

Dr. Martin Keller arrived in the trauma bay unsure of what the moment would produce and unaware that a critical instrument he recently had requested had arrived the previous week. After assessing the surgery and emergency departments,

Keller had questioned the hospital's preparedness and dedication to trauma. One omission he noted was the absence of a Lebsche knife. He had long considered the tool, with the look of a shiny, miniature putter, a necessary option for the rare occasions it was needed to quickly slice into the chest of a trauma patient on the brink of death. And now, there it was, tucked inconspicuously into a tray where it could be accessed at a moment's notice.

The knife, a combination of blade and chisel, was waiting when Trevin was wheeled into the emergency room. The bullet entered at his nipple line, pierced the lower lobe of his left lung and damaged a major blood vessel before exiting through his back. Emergency medical technicians had the situation under control until entering the ambulance garage at the hospital. At that point, his vitals crashed. Simultaneously pushing the gurney carrying the 150-pound boy and thrusting at his chest, paramedics took the first left turn inside the hospital doors into the trauma bay. Waiting was a growing throng of nurses, emergency department physicians, surgeons, anesthesiologists, residents and medical students, who sensed something out of the ordinary was about to unfold.

Keller was informed that Trevin's status had taken the worst turn possible. He decided the only option was to perform an emergency thoracotomy, in which an incision is made across a patient's sternum and the chest pried open to expose the heart and other vital organs. There wasn't time for a trip to the operating room. It is a quick and messy procedure done on the spot. On another occasion when Keller opened a chest in the emergency room, the outcome came swiftly. He performed a thoracotomy on a gunshot victim only to find that the tip of the heart had been blown away. That patient had no chance.

Trevin was doused with Betadine, a brownish-yellow disinfectant and rolled slightly to provide a view of his back. A hole in line with the chest wound was apparent, indicating that the likelihood of a retained bullet was low. Previously the chest would have been opened with a tool strong enough to cut through a child's chest but lacking for someone Trevin's size. Instead, Keller grabbed the Lebsche knife. One year after his arrival from a neighboring hospital, he embarked on a case that would allow everyone involved to pass judgment on his reputation as a top-rate trauma surgeon.

Keller began by making an incision starting with the sternum at the fifth rib and extending downward to the side of the bed. Alternately cutting and pounding, he sliced through the bony portion of the chest and within minutes had created the needed opening, into which a retractor was placed and then cranked to separate the ribs and expose the organs to which Keller and the trauma team required access. Trevin's chest was filled with blood, making the injuries difficult to evaluate. Keller requested a suction device and watched as trauma manager and longtime nurse Diana Kraus, wearing slacks and a dress shirt, reached for the floor. In the midst of the chaos, it had fallen. Without another at the ready, Keller invoked the five-second rule typically reserved for a fumbled cookie.

"I'm just using it," he said. "If he gets an infection and we're dealing with that down the road, we probably had a good day."

With the field temporarily cleared, Keller could see the bullet had missed Trevin's heart. But his lung was bleeding profusely, and the danger of bleeding to death without reaching the operating room was a looming possibility. The bullet had passed through a portion of the hilum, where arteries, veins and vessels enter the lung. He reached into the teen's chest, took the left lung in both hands and twisted the lower lobe over the upper lobe. The maneuver, known as a pulmonary hilum twist, is used to control hemorrhaging in severe lung trauma. It has an effect similar to a garden hose becoming twisted, cutting off the flow of water. He clamped the hilum and returned his attention to Trevin's heart, which was quivering but not beating.

The sac around the heart was opened. Keller clamped the aorta with the hope of sending remaining blood to the brain. He grabbed an internal defibrillator and placed the tiny pads on each side of the heart, delivering a jolt equal to 10 joules. A surgery fellow, meanwhile, massaged the heart with great care to avoid damage. Epinephrine was injected directly into the heart to increase the contraction rate and improve blood flow. All the while, Trevin was undergoing a massive transfusion, ultimately losing about half of his blood and receiving 10 units. The combination of twisting, massaging, jump-starting and injecting had given him a second chance.

No more than 20 minutes had passed since Trevin entered the room. Everything had gone as well as could be expected, with the possible exception of the dropped suction tube; at this point it seemed a minor issue. Trevin was still in danger, but he had been resuscitated and was going to survive the emergency room for a trip to the sixth floor, where a more quiet and sterile operating room awaited.

The resuscitation had gone so well that Keller would count among his most vivid memories an odd moment of levity. The scene in a trauma bay for a gunshot wound can be hectic at best, descending to gory and out of control in the midst of the action. The ER was packed for Trevin. The floor was splattered with his blood. His chest was gaping. At one point in the middle of the mayhem but after the patient had been stabilized, Keller looked up to catch a glimpse of the chief resident. He was dressed in white, waving his arms and yelling, "We need calm in here." It was a ham-handed attempt to help in some small way, but Keller only remembers it as unintended humor and a slight break in the tension.

"Your sphincter is pretty tight when you get involved in this," Keller said. "I look up, he's dressed in white and yelling. I'm thinking, 'You've got to be kidding me.' It was almost like 'Animal House' when they're having the parade, and one guy in a military outfit yells, 'Remain calm! All is well!' He meant well, and the timing was perfect."

Keller has a knack for drawing parallels between work scenarios and pop culture, from 1960s album cover art to "Seinfeld" minutia and anything Grateful Dead. He compared the scene in the trauma bay that day to the crowd on the crowded cover of the Beatles' album "Sgt. Pepper's Lonely Hearts Club Band." He's also a master of self-deprecation, and his response to the success in giving Trevin a chance for survival was no different.

"Every once in a while you fumble your way through," he said.

What transpired was, in many ways, what was envisioned when Keller joined the staff as director of trauma. He was hired in 2007, making the three-mile move from Cardinal Glennon Children's Hospital. His transition came as St. Louis was racking up enough gun deaths in 2006 and 2007 among kids ranging in age from 10 to 19 to rank second nationally for that age group. The city's rate of 50 firearm homicides per 100,000 residents trailed only New Orleans. Many argued the rating was misleading because it included the city of St. Louis but not the dozens of surrounding municipalities that make up St. Louis County. But the fact remained that gun incidents, whether acts of violence, accidents or self-inflicted, were on the rise as Keller was delving into his new job. His directive was to improve treatment, even reduce the number of gunshot wounds coming through the doors. The timing for this challenge couldn't have been more perfect.

St. Louis Children's Hospital, like Cardinal Glennon, is a Level 1 pediatric trauma center, but the volume of gunshot patients is greater at SLCH. The hospital sits on Kingshighway Boulevard, a major arterial road that passes through the northern high-crime portion of the city, past hospitals and medical facilities that border sprawling Forest Park in the central corridor and through south St. Louis. SLCH also is a quick hop from Interstate 64, which runs east and west and splits the St. Louis metropolitan area down the middle.

One of Keller's responsibilities upon being hired was to improve the hospital's status as a trauma center. He had completed a fellowship in trauma and critical care at Children's Hospital of Philadelphia and ran the show at Cardinal Glennon. Now he was entering a hospital where top-of-the-line trauma service was imperative, particularly considering that 986 gunshot wound (GSW) victims would be seen from 2005 to 2017. That doesn't include more than 300 murder victims ages 19 and younger in the city of St. Louis during the same period. Many such kids generally don't make it to the hospital to have a chance at survival.

The major thrust of Keller's initial undertaking was to gain verification for the hospital from the American College of Surgeons. The ACS program was established to highlight facilities that have the resources to offer optimal trauma care, and SLCH was lacking in some areas. He faced the daunting task of navigating hospital bureaucracy to streamline systems and improve treatment. Additional staffing was needed to meet the require-

ments. There was a need to forge a better working relationship between the wide-ranging personalities in the emergency
and surgery departments. And there were plenty of housekeep-
ing tasks, such as securing a Lebsche knife. The acquisition
wasn't a groundbreaking decision, just part of the nuts and bolts
necessary for improvement.

"In 2007 or 2008 we had several patients shot in the chest,
and the likelihood of death is 40 percent," said Kraus, the hospital's longtime trauma manager. "We would have patients
come in, and we did not do a good job. We might have gotten
them to the operating room to give them a chance. Now we save
them. We put the pieces into place. The first time Marty opened
a chest here, he didn't have the knife. Marty has trauma training and said, 'No, we have to have it.'"

Emergency room thoracotomies remain a last resort. When
performed, the survival rate for pediatric victims of penetrating
injuries — generally gun or knife wounds — is 12 percent. In
the wake of Trevin's case, Keller's decision to perform the dramatic procedure was questioned. But this was not an unusual
scenario for a GSW. These cases are not like the planned surgeries Keller and his colleagues perform on a daily basis. They
are sudden, accompanied by little advance notice and require
instantaneous decision making based on what ends up in the
trauma bay. The information provided by paramedics might be
accurate. But it's not unusual for a patient to arrive under a set
of circumstances quite different than first described when the ambulance is en route.

Trevin's survival remained uncertain after the thoracotomy,
but he made it to the OR, where the drama subsided. Keller
performed a lobectomy to remove the lower portion of the left
lung. After arriving at the hospital at 3:35 p.m. with virtually no

signs of life, Trevin was wheeled into the intensive care unit at 6:45.

Keller saw Trevin during rounds every day for the next 42 days. Personnel from neurology suggested he was brain dead. Some felt that keeping him on life support was futile. Keller disagreed, believing that Trevin was "locked in," meaning he could sense activity or sensations without the ability to react. There were occasional changes in vital signs when Trevin was touched. Two weeks after surgery, Keller performed a tracheostomy and inserted a feeding tube to allow for long-term care.

"If he's aware and can't move, that's got to be worse than not aware," Keller said. "Imagine you're sitting there, taped down to the bed, and you can't move or even scratch yourself if you itch. That's got to be the worst thing ever. That's what I thought he had because he was responding to some of my exams."

Eventually, Trevin was sent to Ranken Jordan, a pediatric specialty hospital in St. Louis County where patients transition from hospital care to their homes. The notes accompanying his release offered virtually no hope.

"Devastating anoxic brain injury left him with little to no independent function," a nurse at SLCH wrote. "Non-communicative, non-responsive, no purposeful movements."

Keller knew the survival rate for the procedures he and his colleagues had performed was extremely low. Trevin was not expected to live.

"Everyone kept saying, 'Why did we do this? This is stupid,'" trauma nurse practitioner Mary Alice McCubbins said.

After Trevin was transferred, the holiday season arrived, winter kicked in and the calendar flipped to a new year. Keller was sitting in his office in January when his phone rang. On the other end was Barb Champion, a former SLCH nurse who had moved to Ranken Jordan. Trevin, she told him, was awake and alert. Despite Keller's confidence that there had been some sliver of hope, he was shocked. He saw Trevin in his trauma clinic Jan. 20. The notes after the exam told a surprising story:

"Has had remarkable progress, becoming much more interactive. He's now able to answer questions. Visual acuity is still questionable. Hearing is intact. He responds to his mother's questions. Ambulate with assistance and has made remarkable progress with rehabilitation."

Had the case occurred a year earlier, Keller couldn't say that Trevin would have survived. It would have taken longer to open his chest. It also was fortuitous for everyone involved that the shooting happened the day following the hospital's successful state review. Everything was in its proper place, everyone well-versed on procedures.

"When I got to Children's I wasn't convinced that they could pass the state review," Keller said. "I didn't tell anybody that. There was so much that wasn't in place. There was no one interested in trauma, and they were running on fumes at that point. If you'd pinned down the right people, they would have said we were in trouble. A year earlier I don't know if we would have been as skilled."

In the face of much doubt and questioning, Keller quietly enjoyed a degree of satisfaction from Trevin's recovery. Four years later the teen returned to have his gallbladder removed, and Keller was assigned the case. Over time, when Keller gave lectures, he used a slide show that concluded with a picture of Trevin and his mother.

"When the job gets a little crappy and you wonder if anything is going right," Keller said, "you think about those kids."

* * *

My earliest conversations with Keller were on the sidelines of many youth soccer, basketball and baseball games. But I first learned about his work through others. The guy in the University of Pennsylvania cap, cargo shorts and sandals did not talk about his job and didn't have the look of someone who saved lives.

As a journalist working for the St. Louis Post-Dispatch and other newspapers, I've spent decades in newsrooms where the steady toll of gun violence is piped in around the clock through police scanners. My direct connection to that violence was muted. I'm a sportswriter, not a crime reporter.

But when the number of children being injured by guns began to surge, Keller became vocal about what he was seeing. The idea to document how a children's hospital handled what seemed an adult problem provided an opportunity to see a side of St. Louis that many prefer not to think about. It is a vantage point that Keller has had for a decade. I was given access to some of the workings of a hospital taking on an extraordinary and disproportionate load of gunshot injuries.

I was tethered to that trauma by Keller, who agreed to alert me, when possible, to child and adolescent gunshot cases as they occurred over the course of several years. His text messages at all hours of the day and night portrayed the sometimes dizzying and tiring pace kept by surgeons and the rest of the staff. Ultimately, they allowed me to witness the medical team at work and parents as they came to grips with their children's serious injuries at a violent crossroads in the middle of America.

This is the story not only of Keller but of many doctors and staff who have navigated a hospital through the tumult and agony of individual gunshot cases. It's the story of a hospital tackling challenging questions of how best to serve those kids, including the rather vexing matter of who, according to age, should be treated at a children's hospital.

To follow Keller is to better understand how doctors and an entire hospital are tested to the limits of their ability as they extract, one by one, the bullets of an American epidemic. Following the trail of those bullets took me deeper than I had expected. It led to lives bruised and destroyed, such as that of a young man shot while walking to high school and a mother whose 12-year-old son went to play at a friend's house but ended up dead.

Along the way, my understanding of shootings that impact children and adolescents expanded far beyond my image of wayward older teens, hardened by gangs, drugs and retribution. Shootings born of those factors are abundant, of course, feeding St. Louis Children's Hospital with more than its share of trauma. But the toll of guns is measured, as well, by the sheer inherent dangers. Many cases are due to guns being left accessible during a typical day.

There was an incident in which a young boy found a shotgun and shot his brother while their father smoked marijuana in another room; a 4-year-old either shot himself or was shot in the stomach by a 5-year-old, according to conflicting stories from his family; a 2-year-old boy was left paralyzed after his father's gun accidentally discharged; a 6-year-old girl was shot in the midsection by her brother, who had pulled a loaded gun off a rack as their mother watched helplessly; a 15-year-old girl was shot and killed by her 20-year-old brother after he found a gun that had been spray-painted gold and mistook it for a toy; a 4-year-old accustomed to drinking water from a water pistol found a loaded gun, placed it in his mouth and pulled the trigger; a 3-year-old found a gun between two mattresses and shot himself in the head; a 13-year-old accidentally shot herself in the side — one of three shootings involving children in a matter of hours on the same day; the 3-year-old son of a St. Louis County police officer found a gun in his home and killed himself with a single blast; and a 2-year-old found a gun on a bed and shot his father in the neck as he slept, killing him. The list goes on and on.

"It's all nuts to me," Keller said. "There are so many stupid stories."

Together, Keller, his fellow surgeons and staff throughout SLCH helped flesh out those stories and the story of a hospital battling an extraordinary decade of violence — one that would bring more gun-wounded children through its doors than any time in the hospital's history.

The Mission

To enter St. Louis Children's Hospital is to step into a world bombarded with audacious, never-ending color and decorative props, starting the moment you reach the parking garage.

Whimsical sculptures by artist Charles Houska dot the winding path through the structure's seven levels, each designated by a zoo animal. A child's voice greets you on the elevator and assures you of your location at each stop. Arriving on the second floor, you encounter an elevated electric train, running on rails in a hall that leads to one of the hospital's main lobbies. The adjacent atrium cafeteria is dominated by a three-story replica hot-air balloon adorned with pink, yellow, orange and purple banners. The dining chairs are nearly neon, and eye-popping yellow umbrellas hang over the tables. The walls, and even the carpets, indiscriminately shift from one luminescent color to another.

The interior decorator's target audience was pre-teen. No color was spared to brighten the days of patients and their families until they hopefully are able to leave with health fully restored.

But there are cases that don't fit neatly into the child demographic. The comforting aesthetic of youthful innocence can belie the grown-up brutality that sometimes turns up in the emergency room. In responding, SLCH has pushed the boundaries of who a children's hospital should serve, setting it apart from most peer hospitals in the United States.

Such was the situation when a robbery turned deadly at a restaurant in downtown St. Louis. One of the perpetrators shot and killed a bartender and then experienced instant karma when he was struck in the chest by an errant bullet fired by one of his cohorts. Minutes later, a car screeched to a stop at the entrance to the ER. The man who had just played a role in a fatal shooting was dumped at the doorstep. The driver fled.

When Dr. Patrick Dillon entered the trauma bay, Dr. Kathryn Bernabe already was hovering over the victim's open chest. She had clamped vessels to control the bleeding, and the patient was rushed to an operating room in an attempt to save his life. Ultimately, his heart was damaged beyond repair, and he died on the table. When Dillon's head cleared, he thought more closely about what he had seen.

"I remembered looking at the guy in the ER and thinking that, sure, we see older kids," he said. "But he had a receding hairline."

The man who had been unceremoniously discarded at the hospital turned out to be 30 years old. More than likely, his buddy didn't realize he had hastily stopped at the children's hospital instead of the emergency entrance at Barnes-Jewish Hospital less than 100 yards away. Or the decision could have been strategic, with security and police seemingly less of a risk at SLCH than at the adult hospital. In terms of medical care, the choice didn't matter.

Physicians at SLCH are well-versed in trauma and handle more than the norm when it comes to gunshot wounds, known as GSWs to medical personnel. Additionally, SLCH has long maintained a policy to treat anyone who comes through the doors, regardless of age or background. The arrival of a patient who turned out to be 30 and a potential murder suspect was highly unusual, but the willingness of Bernabe and Dillon to take action said as much about the simple concept of treating the sick and injured as it did the hospital's mission.

When it comes to penetrating injuries, and more specifically gunshot wounds, SLCH treats an 18-year-old gang member injured in a drive-by shooting much the same as a 4-year-old accidentally wounded by a friend. It's an approach that few children's hospitals embrace and one that has put the hospital consistently above the national rate of GSWs. In 2006, 9.9 percent of the hospital's trauma admissions were for GSWs. The number rose to 10 percent in 2007, 13.9 percent in 2008 and 11.1 percent in 2009. According to the American College of Surgeons' annual trauma reports, the national average was never higher than 5.8 percent during those years. Whereas the state of Missouri mandates only that the hospital accept patients up to age 15, the official cut-off at SLCH is 21. That age has been surpassed many times.

The hospital's philosophy is simple. Accept anyone. Accumulate a wealth of experience by treating GSWs suffered by older victims to better handle all ages. Have victims admitted to the hospital so that they receive access to social services to address issues that may have led to the shootings. Most important, reduce the number of kids being shot. It's a public health approach to guns and a concept that comes with a considerable amount of scrutiny.

"We've changed our approach," Keller said of his tenure. "We're more active in recognizing it's a major health problem in the city. We've taken the approach that prevention is probably the best medicine."

SLCH's guidelines on age have created a debate. Once a hospital starts accepting kids in their middle and upper teens, the number of cases it takes involving violence and gangs increases. So it is not surprising that it is most common for medical facilities to stop taking pediatric trauma patients when they reach their 14th or 15th birthdays. Some children's hospitals don't take trauma patients after they reach their teen years.

For many years, Comer Children's Hospital in Chicago didn't accept trauma patients older than 15. That practice led to protests on the city's south side in 2013 as community members fought to have the trauma unit increase its age limit due to the lack of a similar facility for adults in that area of the city. They believed the lack of treatment for those 16 and older was costing people their lives. Because of that limit, 18-year-old youth activist Damian Turner was taken 10 miles to Northwestern Memorial Hospital when he was shot in August 2010. He bled to death, and many blamed his outcome on the age limit at Comer. In December 2014, the hospital announced that it would expand the trauma program to accept patients until their 18th birthday.

Hospitals that accept traumas into the late teen years are the exception. That is why Keller said he receives looks of disbelief when he speaks at conferences as his peers wonder why SLCH opens itself to so much penetrating trauma.

SLCH opened in 1879 and is the oldest pediatric hospital west of the Mississippi River. In the early days, the guidelines for admittance were far more restrictive. The annual report in 1880 set forth the basic ground rules: "Patients between the ages of two and fourteen, suffering from acute diseases, medical or surgical, are received at the Hospital. No patient is admitted whose case is considered chronic or incurable, unless in the opinion of the staff relief can be given."

Over time, the rules relaxed. The practice of taking older GSW patients has been in place longer than anyone can remember.

If a change was going to be considered, Dr. Brad Warner nipped that in the bud when he arrived as surgeon-in-chief in 2007. He re-emphasized the idea that age, socioeconomic status and even suspicion of unlawful activity are never grounds for rejection.

"If we isolate gunshots to what we consider the kid population – no facial hair, no tattoos, no bling – our numbers would go way down," he said. "So I think by extending it to teenagers we do a better job for the kids that come here. Our experience level is greater, and the systems have all been well-oiled and the kinks worked out. That came up when we had a gunshot to an 18-year-old. Everyone was real upset that we took this guy, who obviously had gang ties, tattoos and a lot of stuff going on. It kind of spooked a lot of people who choose to work in a children's hospital, and I understand that. But for all the griping we heard, the very next day we had a stab wound in a 4-year-old. What we learned systemwide from that 18-year-old can apply to the 4-year-old.

"There is a conflict there, and that's something inherent in what we do. We go into medicine not to choose to take care of the people who can pay. We don't go into medicine to only operate on people who have a job or lifestyle that agrees with what we consider our values. It's not fair to treat anyone differently based on what bad decisions they've made or what they were born into from a socioeconomic status."

Warner brought that belief from Cincinnati Children's Hospital, where he had worked for 25 years. He was lured to SLCH after considering numerous chief-of-surgery positions around the country. His hiring was considered a bit of a coup. Not only was the hospital gaining a respected and in-demand surgeon but a personality willing to be the face of pediatric surgery. While Keller and others can't run fast enough from cameras, Warner doesn't shy away. In 2013, he was featured in a local six-episode television series, "Frontline for Hope," a documentary-style look at a variety of cases at the hospital. During its run, Warner's face was front and center on a banner plastered high above the main entrance to the hospital. He has the friendly personality a camera loves and a gentle voice and easy smile that any parent would appreciate in a tense situation.

But "Frontline for Hope" didn't document any gunshot wounds. That came as no surprise to Keller, who is accustomed to television crews and newspapers featuring rare diseases, the arrival of children from other countries or kids stricken with cancer. One of his common refrains is that you will never see a telethon to raise money for the epidemic of gun injuries and deaths among children.

"There's a belief that they're all gang-bangers or deserved it somehow, and that's not the case," Keller said. "But that's the way it gets interpreted, so it doesn't generate the same level of empathy, the warm and fuzzies. That's a hard thing because even in this hospital some people are questioning why we're so involved in the care of these patients."

For a long time, that list included Dillon, who has known Keller since their days working together at Cardinal Glennon in the late 1990s. Before arriving in St. Louis, Dillon completed a fellowship in pediatric surgery at Johns Hopkins. That's where he was ingrained with the idea that if you're shot and at least 15, you go to an adult hospital. He admits that the arrival of an 18-year-old still gives him pause and reason to contemplate, "Is this why I went into pediatric surgery?" But ultimately, his desire to help kids is too strong for him to suggest it is anything more than an annoyance.

Nevertheless, he is quick to point out that the only reason he had to be in the ER with the 30-year-old shooting victim was that Keller was stuck in Puerto Rico, his flight home from a conference having been canceled. Keller was scheduled to be on call that night. But the two have a good relationship. Dillon helped to train Keller at Cardinal Glennon. They are office neighbors. Both spent time at Ivy League schools, share a discomfort with media attention and are running aficionados. Their relationship and similar interests have softened Dillon, to a degree.

"For the greater good of the program and knowing what Marty and Brad want to accomplish, I've become a little more tolerant," he said.

Once Keller arrived, Dillon had little choice but to accept an older GSW population, if only for his sanity. From 2008 to 2016, 46 percent of GSW patients at the hospital were 16 or older, although the average age has been trending significantly downward. It is not unusual for the hospital to have patients in their 20s show up with gun injuries.

SLCH's central location and the geography of St. Louis make the hospital an ideal candidate to handle the overload. The hospital is part of a medical campus that spans several square blocks. Barnes-Jewish Hospital is a neighbor to the south. The 164 acres of prime real estate also include Siteman Cancer Center, Goldfarb School of Nursing Barnes-Jewish College, Central Institute for the Deaf, St. Louis College of Pharmacy and numerous other research centers, medical facilities and parking garages.

The campus is framed by a diverse and eclectic mix of landscapes. To the west sit 1,371 acres of Forest Park, which hosted the 1904 World's Fair. It now encompasses museums, a world-class zoo, an outdoor theater, softball fields, a golf course, restaurants and a meandering system of running and biking paths. To the east is a view of the Gateway Arch and downtown St. Louis in the distance, the five miles between filled with a mix of classic architecture and ramshackle buildings. Directly north is the Central West End, an eating and drinking hub and home to myriad mansions. Tennessee Williams grew up here, and poet T.S. Eliot and beat writer William Burroughs lived in homes in the historic district. To the south is The Grove neighborhood and entertainment district, especially popular with the city's gay and lesbian community.

Communities north and east of the Central West End are major contributors to the high level of GSWs. The 63112, 63113, 63115 and 63136 ZIP codes sent 173 GSW victims to the hospital from 2008 to 2016. During the bulk of that time, about 27,000 children lived within the boundaries of the city's then-unaccredited school district. When Superintendent Kelvin Adams was hired in 2007, the district had a 50 percent graduation rate. The city was experiencing hard times, and it was reflected in the steady stream of gun injuries. By that time, paramedics had been well-versed in the practice of taking many who appeared to be in their teen years to SLCH.

Kate Bernabe, one of the hospital's surgeons, never considered that older kids should go elsewhere. She spent her residency in New Orleans at a community hospital that saw virtually no penetrating trauma and thus no GSWs. When she started her fellowship at SLCH in the fall of 2008, she didn't question the practice of taking older gunshot victims. Bernabe, a mother of three, never wavered from that stance even after experiencing the heavy caseload. Despite enduring some of the hospital's busiest years, she didn't hesitate when she was offered a spot on the surgical staff.

She viewed working alongside Keller as the perfect gateway to understanding the treatment of GSWs. She was accustomed to operating on 18-year-olds with other ailments, so handling their penetrating wounds made sense as a transition to working on younger patients. In doing so, she eventually heard some of the grousing but never bothered to ask why a hospital caregiver would feel that way. But she has a theory.

"If you aren't used to taking care of gunshot wounds, you feel uncomfortable in those situations," she said. "So, I don't think they want to deal with gunshot wounds regardless of the age. Once the surgeon does an operation, it's the surgeon who has the most contact with that person in the hospital. The surgeon is taking care of rounding with that patient. If we don't mind taking care of those patients, everything should be hunky dory."

Accepting older patients takes SLCH into a different territory. It is not something the hospital publicizes because, as several people told me, some parents are not comfortable having their sons or daughters, with their tonsils just removed, in close proximity to someone recovering from a GSW.

Dr. David Jaffe, who was the hospital's longtime director for emergency services until his departure in 2015, supported the all-ages policy from the start. Few have been involved in pediatric emergency medicine longer than Jaffe, who was one of the first pediatric emergency medicine fellows in the country. Three decades of watching GSWs pass through the doors at SLCH did nothing to sway his opinion.

"The hospital has an age cut-off of the 21st birthday for the rest of its services, and I've always believed that should be the case for emergency services," he said. "Making an exception for a specific kind of injury or illness didn't make a whole lot of sense to me. The care of youth in their teen years is a challenge for a variety of reasons. But there is evidence to show that in terms of social, emotional and intellectual development that pediatrics is more appropriate, even in the upper teen years. The capability to handle the context to violence in which some of these occur presents a challenge for a children's hospital, and I get that."

Numerous studies have attempted to determine if younger patients actually have better outcomes at children's hospitals or if they can be served just as well at adult hospitals, including those with pediatric wings.

A large study published in 2006 looked at 79,673 injury cases. The Medical College of Wisconsin, Children's Research Institute and American Pediatric Surgical Association in Milwaukee looked at in-hospital mortality, length of stay and costs. Researchers determined that 89 percent of these cases did not involve treatment at a children's hospital. However, the outcomes in all three areas were better at children's hospitals. The mortality rate at children's hospitals was 0.9 percent compared to 1.4 percent at adult hospitals and 2.4 percent at adult hospitals with a children's unit. Length of stay and cost of care were both lower at children's hospitals.

"Because of their unique physiology, children have particular needs and present challenges to predominantly adult-oriented trauma care delivery systems," lead researcher John C. Densmore said.

Douglas Schuerer, a surgeon and head of the trauma department at Barnes-Jewish, doesn't necessarily see it that way. His hospital handles about 500 gunshot patients every year, and a large chunk of those are kids age 15 and older. Schuerer has experience in pediatrics. He completed a year of pediatric training at the University of Michigan and then saw a considerable amount of adult and children's penetrating trauma at Henry Ford Hospital in Detroit. He is at ease in handling younger patients.

"We've always said we'd take the older kids," Schuerer said. "In fact, in a lot of ways those 16-, 18-year-olds just fit in better here. That's probably true. But Children's didn't want people to feel they weren't taking care of a certain population. The community wants to know you can take care of everybody.

"I've always pushed for 15 and over to come here. I don't care what the cause. It doesn't have to be gang violence. I don't think anyone in the world would think less of Children's Hospital. I think those guys are happy to take care of it, but if we said tomorrow we'd take it all, they'd kind of be OK with it."

Studies are inconclusive as to whether pediatric trauma centers are better for children. The University of Arizona conducted research involving more than 45,000 injuries. The mortality rate at children's hospitals was shown to be a full percent lower, but the study concluded that the difference was not statistically significant.

The University of Southern California and Children's Hospital of Los Angeles sought to determine if there was a difference in outcomes between pediatric trauma centers and adult trauma centers that possess qualifications to treat injured children. The results were inconclusive. The research did, however, determine that there was some evidence of lower mortality rates and better nonoperative outcomes at children's trauma centers.

The bottom line is that the minimal number of pediatric trauma centers nationally necessitates that many children be treated at adult hospitals. The debate about which produces better outcomes is likely to persist. Sometimes, there simply is not enough time to send someone from SLCH to Barnes-Jewish, or vice versa, if that patient arrives and needs immediate care.

* * *

When 20-year-old Kendell Jones appeared at SLCH's ER on a summer night in 2013 with a bullet wound in his back, he was greeted by medical and security personnel. The car carrying Kendell and some friends was riddled with bullet holes. It's the type of case that causes considerable wringing of hands.

No one at the hospital could make an immediate and informed decision as to whether Kendell and his friends had been involved in wrongdoing or targeted for no reason. The only thing they knew was that he needed treatment. Meanwhile, police became involved while other families were coming and going from the ER with children.

In the end, he was fine. He returned a few weeks later and told me of his ongoing pain from the bullet, which an X-ray showed was sitting upright atop his left shoulder. Kendell was curled in an exam room chair, a jacket draped across his body.

"We were just outside the car talking," Kendell said of the night he was shot. "We took off, went around a corner and a car was chasing us. We hit the alley and that's when they got to shooting. They shot into the car, and one came through the trunk and hit me in the back. They rushed me to the hospital. I was dying in the car. I was at the wrong place at the wrong time. For real."

A date for the 15-minute procedure to remove the bullet was scheduled. But Kendell never made it because he landed in jail.

Dark Days

To say there were times during Dr. Pat Dillon's long tenure at St. Louis Children's Hospital that tested his patience would be an understatement. Considered by some to be a bit ornery, he is tall and lanky and strikes an imposing figure. Dillon has worked at the hospital for all but a few years in the past three decades. For many of those years, he did not embrace the idea of taking all ages of gunshot victims. His disdain became known to many in the hospital. Why not send them to the adult hospital? It's a question he asked repeatedly. His line of thinking was shared by others who saw such patients as not only on the brink of adulthood but involved in shootings often tied to adult-like activities.

"It just made me sort of frustrated sometimes when I went down there, saw a patient and went, 'Really?'" Dillon said. "When I would bring it up, people would look at me like I was crazy. Like, how could we ever turn away this 18-year-old drug dealer? Pretty easily. Look around the country and there are plenty of hospitals that have done it successfully."

Over three decades, Dillon has witnessed the progression of patients with gunshot wounds in St. Louis. He watched as SLCH was bombarded in the early '90s before he left to work for two years at Johns Hopkins Hospital in Baltimore. He returned to St. Louis in 1997, joining the staff at nearby Cardinal Glennon. That is where he first got to know Keller, who was starting a fellowship. Before long, however, Dillon found his way back to SLCH in 1999.

His return came at the start of a rather tumultuous period as challenges escalated in the years that followed. The hospital struggled to maintain a consistent surgical staff. That shortage was felt amid the effort to offer proper care for trauma cases, which continued to climb. It was a period that tested the commitment to serving all gunshot victims, almost to a breaking point. It was also a period in which Dillon intensified his effort to recruit someone he knew could be a key player in stabilizing the ship: Keller, his former colleague at Cardinal Glennon.

Dillon's desire to send some shooting victims elsewhere — or at least reconsider the policy on the issue — was understandable given the state of hospital in 1999 and the years that followed. Surgeons came and went for years until Dillon essentially was the only person remaining to handle trauma cases while also juggling a burgeoning daily caseload of scheduled surgeries.

It's not what he had envisioned. He felt the long-term potential was better at SLCH. He suspected the surgical staff had a better chance for growth and stability. Dillon's departure left Cardinal Glennon with two surgeons and boosted SLCH to three. The volume of trauma cases, specifically GSWs, was fairly stable at that point, and the staff was large enough to spread the work without anyone feeling overwhelmed. That soon changed.

Diana Kraus also was frustrated by the fluctuations in staffing and commitment to trauma during her 21 years at SLCH. She finished her tenure as the trauma program manager, a position she held for eight years. She had watched as the system grew, stumbled and stagnated while working in a variety of roles and from an array of perspectives. During much of her time, trauma simply wasn't a priority but more of a burdensome necessity that no one seemed willing to embrace. She worked in the Barnes-Jewish emergency room from 1985 to 1993, a period known among medical personnel as the "knife and gun club" for its escalation of gang violence. She moved to SLCH while working as a nurse to escape that environment.

"At that time there wasn't a lot of good training," she said. "The philosophy was you learn as you go. I had a three-day orientation at Children's, and you swam or sank. Traditionally, you're with someone for six weeks. They show you how to do it – the protocols and services. I was with someone for three days. I look back and think, 'What was I doing?'"

Dillon and Kraus viewed the surgery department of the early 2000s as a dysfunctional family. Dillon joined the team when Robert Foglia was the chief of surgery, a position he held from 1990 to 2006. Promising surgeons such as Jacob Langer and Mike Skinner were on their way out, prompting a sequence of hirings and departures that interrupted consistency of the surgical staff. George Mychaliska came aboard in 2001 but stayed for only two years before heading to Ann Arbor, Mich. The hospital again had four surgeons when Tamir Keshen was added, but his tenure also was brief. Rob Minkes left for New Orleans to become chief of pediatric surgery.

"Foglia was getting increasingly frustrated at the administration about not having enough resources to keep people and build the program," Dillon said. "We were constantly between three and four surgeons, and that's not growing the program. You're not getting the continuity you want."

During this period the hospital convened what was known as the Blue Ribbon Commission. It was comprised of two outside surgeons and one from within. Commission members conducted interviews with everyone in the surgical department and issued a report. The findings sounded a lot like what everyone already had realized, only now they were on paper. More surgeons were necessary along with more resources, which meant more money needed to be spent if SLCH was going to run a division that was healthy and productive. Recruiting efforts had been underway to find additional surgeons, but that effort came to an abrupt halt. Then Foglia left in 2006.

Kraus had just taken over as the hospital's trauma program manager, a position she held from 2005 to 2013. She previously worked as a transport nurse, charge nurse and nurse supervisor. She had a big personality and brought immense confidence and sass to the job. Kraus tended to be out front on many issues during her managerial years, and her viewpoints were rarely left unstated.

She pointed to personality conflicts as a significant factor in the constant turnover among surgeons. She, along with others, said there was a significant rift between the surgery and emergency departments. Arguments in trauma committee meetings were not uncommon as a power struggle unfolded.

"The attitude was, 'I've just got to get through the day.' No one embraced trauma whatsoever. It was contentious," Kraus said. "There was this culture of teaching future surgeons to be assholes. And they were, and they treated the ER staff like that. It was fragmented, and people didn't work together. If you don't have people communicating, you're not going to do a good job of handing off patient care."

* * *

Dillon felt a twinge of promise when SLCH first contacted Brad Warner, who was working in Cincinnati and considered a target for any children's hospital in need of a chief of surgery. But Dillon quickly developed the feeling that Warner's vision might be too grandiose for hospital administrators. They met for lunch at a convention in 2005 and Dillon walked away with one impression: "He's not coming, and this is a big problem."

In the meantime, another surgeon was about to leave in the summer of 2006, and Dillon was facing the prospect of being on his own. The idea was preposterous. Having one general surgeon at the city's largest children's hospital could make for the type of situation that might drive patients away if it were to become public. The prospect was bad enough even without knowing that the number of gunshot wounds was about to explode. In an attempt to patch the wound until it could heal, an acquaintance arranged a meeting between Dillon and Dr. Dick Bower, who was nearing retirement. Bower joined the faculty at Washington University School of Medicine in 1977 and went on to become an SLCH surgeon until 1990, when he left for Florida. He returned to St. Louis at Cardinal Glennon in 2000. And now, Dillon and Bower were chatting over beers at Tom's Bar and Grill, a short walk from SLCH, and discussing what it would take for Bower to finish his career where he had started. He bit.

The hospital had two surgeons as of the summer of 2006 and was still looking for a chief of surgery. There were clear restrictions on the daily routine. Elective surgeries were limited to specific days. Dillon and Bower split call duty. Meetings and teaching responsibilities were dramatically reduced. The surgery department was in survival mode. Dillon received a bump in his salary, but he also knew that Warner had declined an initial offer.

All the while, technical issues needed to be addressed regarding the treatment of GSWs. Trauma training among the support staff was minimal until new programs were introduced to get people up to speed. The blood bank wasn't at full capacity. Thus, the hospital studied, created and implemented a new mass transfusion system. Necessary equipment upgrades were identified and led to the addition of new rapid infusers, which are critical to infuse warm blood and fluids into patients. As late as 2009, the emergency department CT scanner — the only one in the hospital — was broken for more than a month. The backup plan was to take patients down the street to Barnes-Jewish. Finally, the hospital purchased a second scanner.

Amid the chaos, Dillon was searching for other ways to make life easier. The most logical option, he determined, was for older trauma patients to go to Barnes-Jewish. By this time, Kraus had been hired as the trauma program manager. The two concocted a plan and went about making a presentation to the Children's Medical Executive Committee (CMEC). Meanwhile, GSWs were on the rise. SLCH saw 110 in 2006 at a time when the availability of hands to fix them was limited. The problem became severe enough that the hospital's urologists were asked to be on call as backups for trauma cases. The argument for a change in protocol seemed solid.

The trauma surgeons handle only trauma cases at Barnes-Jewish. Dillon was dealing with patients with GSWs and injuries from motor vehicle accidents while also tackling his other duties, including elective cases. Kraus had to admit that it made sense to at least try to convince the CMEC to alter the hospital's policy.

"I made my presentation and said, 'Look, we're doing everything we can to keep things afloat.' I had talked to the trauma services guys at Barnes, and they were willing to help," Dillon said. "I felt if they took someone who was 16 or 17, they're adult size anyway. It's not like I could say I can take care of this trauma patient better than the adult trauma guys. That's all they're doing every day. You'd have thought I was trying to close the hospital. They said we can't send these kids over there. I was like, 'OK, I tried.'"

What resulted instead was a task force charged with examining how SLCH could better care for older trauma patients. The findings spelled out a long list of needs.

"In the OR, so many things went wrong," Kraus said. "It was simple stuff that no one had paid attention to, and Pat threw a fit. There was no trauma training for the OR staff, so it showed a big gap. We didn't have the right equipment. Some people didn't know how to open defibrillator paddles."

Dr. Nickie Kolovos was placed in charge of the task force, which met for the first time July 18, 2006. The initial recommendations called for:

- A communications center to facilitate incoming calls regarding trauma patients and activate the trauma team.
- A blood refrigerator in the ER trauma room with four units of O-Negative blood.
- Emergency trays by specialty to be kept in trauma rooms. Included were a thoracotomy tray, chest tube insertion tray and central line insertion kit.
- A new CT scanner on the seventh floor, in part as a backup for when the first-floor scanner was unavailable.
- An after-hours OR stocked and ready to accept trauma patients within 10 minutes with no other cases to be assigned to the room after 7 p.m.
- The presence of an OR nurse in the trauma bay when a patient arrives, to better assess needs and the likelihood of going to the OR.
- Consistent use of trauma activation criteria.

"I tried to take the stance that we needed to improve the trauma care provided to any age patient, not just adolescents," Kolovos said. "If we could find ways to provide care for all, it would make it easier to facilitate care for any age.

"In the end, what made it better was having more people. But I think what we were able to achieve was identifying things needed for people of all ages."

That was difficult to envision at the time, especially for Dillon. There were times he was in the OR removing an appendix and a GSW would arrive. Or multiple GSWs would arrive simultaneously.

"My wife would probably tell you I was miserable to live with," Dillon said. "You go home and don't really want to interact with her or the kids. You're dreading that the pager's going to go off. When your wife, who grew up in St. Louis, is ready to say we're putting a for-sale sign in front of the house, that's probably at your limits. But I felt this place had a lot of great potential and felt it was worth sticking it out. I didn't want to wake up one day and wish I'd stayed another six months."

It was the spring of 2007 when Dillon received a call from Lee Fetter, then the president of SLCH. He was flying to Cincinnati to meet with Warner. Warner was going to take the job.

* * *

In 2006, Keller was the last surgeon standing at Cardinal Glennon. He was working virtually every day and on call every night for a run of nine months. Dillon was in similarly dire straits.

"This city was crazy for a couple of years. There was nobody here," Keller said, referring to the shortage of surgeons.

After the failed attempt to send older GSWs to Barnes-Jewish failed, the next option, born of desperation, was to go on diversion. SLCH would occasionally alert paramedics in the field that trauma patients should be taken elsewhere because resources — whether it be beds, surgeons or operating rooms — had been depleted to the point that the hospital couldn't adequately provide care. This option was frowned upon, and hospitals are required to report diversions so that EMS services are aware at any given moment.

"Diversion –- talk about a four-letter word," Dillon says. "But that's what we'd do once in a while. The way I look at diversion is if you reach your capacity to handle any type of patients, you say we can't take any more. You may be running too many ORs on a Saturday night, or the ICU may be so full you couldn't take another patient. It may mean your only surgeon is already doing a case and can't scrub out to go look at somebody else. In my mind, that makes it not real safe to take the next potential trauma."

One especially bad week in 2006 led to a period of complete exhaustion. Keller's breaking point came at the start of a weekend when the prospect of GSWs is highest. On Friday night he determined that business as usual would not be good for himself or patients. Keller called the emergency room and declared a diversion at Cardinal Glennon with no particular end in sight. He needed sleep and wanted temporarily to avoid traumas at all costs. Two nights later, sufficiently recuperated, he ended the diversion. That balancing act continued at the two hospitals as the surgeons tried to stay afloat.

But the never-ending work was taking a toll. Keller was awakened one morning at four o'clock by a call from the emergency room and told that two teenagers in need of appendectomies had been admitted. He had two surgeries scheduled later that day to repair esophageal and intestinal problems in infants – a full day in any surgeon's book. The parents of those babies likely would not have been thrilled to know their surgeon was being asked in the middle of the night to handle procedures that could have been done at numerous hospitals by any number of surgeons.

"I'm yelling at the ER at four in the morning, and my wife is saying 'Stop.' I said, 'I can't stop, I'm so tired,'" Keller recalled. "I liked working at Cardinal Glennon, but it was killing me. I was going to have a heart attack if I kept doing it."

Dillon knew the stress that was building at Cardinal Glennon and figured his friend was ready for a change. But despite the problems, Keller resisted. It took repeated overtures before he agreed to visit SLCH to get an inside look at the facility. He then escaped St. Louis to spend a weekend in Michigan with his family.

All he needed was a little rest, which gave way to a moment of clarity. He awoke one morning and told his wife, Ellen, he was taking the job at Children's.

"I realized what it was like to have a day off, be on vacation, throw a lacrosse ball with my son," he said. "Glennon offered me all kinds of stuff, but I said 'no.' I had to take a long walk to get a signal to make the call. It was time to do something different that didn't involve packing the family and moving."

The Slogger

The roots of Keller's decision to pursue medicine are difficult to trace. His family was not entrenched in the profession, although his mother was a nurse — a job she left when he was born. His father was an accountant. One grandfather was a pharmacist, and there may or may not have been cousins who were doctors. But there was not a definitive medical gene that ran through the family's lineage.

Keller was born in New Haven, Connecticut, in the mid-1960s and grew up in neighboring Branford, a coastal town on Long Island Sound. His early passions were baseball and football. He also loved science. It was a middle-class existence, growing up with a brother and later a sister, who was born when he was 10. His tendency to keep words to a minimum was established early.

"His parents said he would sit in a corner with his toys," Keller's wife, Ellen, said. "And he never said a word."

Keller entered The Hopkins School, a prep school on a hill in New Haven, when he was a high school sophomore. Summers in high school were spent preparing for the next football season. He would run and throw and work a little construction. Although on the short side, Keller was a quarterback. He was a catcher and third baseman on the baseball team but developed tendinitis as a senior and moved to first base because he couldn't lift his arm over his head. At the plate, he had the keen eye of a surgeon, striking out only seven times in three seasons and establishing a school record of reaching base in nine consecutive plate appearances with five hits and four walks.

During his first year at Hopkins, his sister was diagnosed with a brain tumor. Keller was 16 when she died after a year-long battle. At that time, Ellen believes, the initial idea of helping children, possibly in medicine, might have entered Keller's mind.

"He doesn't ever talk about it," she said. "I think that's what motivated him. Either I've felt that for so long I decided that's why, or he told me." Decades later, Keller can't say for sure whether his sister's death spurred him to become a doctor. "I don't know," he said. "I didn't think that way."

However, it wasn't much later that Keller began dabbling in medicine. He secured a pair of intern-like positions during his high school years. He attributed those brief dalliances with the medical field to his parents' attempts to discover where his career interests might lie. The first involved working with his pediatrician, Harold Levy. All that Keller recalls from the experience is examining urine samples under a microscope to determine if they indicated infection. He also volunteered in an emergency room, where he took samples to the lab or wheeled patients to their rooms. Both jobs were simplistic, and Keller never thought at the time that he had found his calling. He certainly knew that construction wasn't in his future. That became obvious when he worked for a contractor, who was a connection through his father. Keller was operating a backhoe one day when he failed to lower the arm and destroyed a garage door. After that he was assigned to basic tasks, such as installing toilet paper holders.

Keller was happy in those years when he was not constrained. It was during those late teen years that he immersed himself in the music of the Grateful Dead. Trips were made with friends down the Eastern seaboard and elsewhere for their concerts. He was laying the groundwork for a lifetime love affair with the Dead's music, to the point that he became most comfortable performing surgery with the group's music playing in the OR.

Keller entered the University of Pennsylvania as a biology major with the idea of becoming a veterinarian. He also wanted to play baseball. Both of those plans failed to materialize, but he found options. One night while sitting in his dorm, Keller received a phone call from Bill Wagner, the coach of Penn's lightweight football program. Now known as sprint football, the varsity sport was for smaller players, who weighed no more than 158 pounds. Keller figured that Wagner must have heard about his high school football career as well as his slight stature.

He joined the team as a backup quarterback. But with seemingly no future at the position due to the presence of an experienced starter, he told Wagner he wanted to switch positions. Keller hit the weight room and returned as a sophomore as the team's fullback, slipping over the weight limit with regularity. "When I came back I'd put on 15 pounds and my dad thought I was on steroids," Keller said. "I had to start making weight by sweating it off."

Football remained part of his college life for four years. The pursuit of a veterinary career, however, ended before he left Penn. He was told by a counselor that he didn't have good enough grades to qualify for vet school and needed to redirect his studies. His roommate and football teammate, John Lopez, planned to pursue medicine. Keller took some of the same courses. When Lopez said he was taking the medical college admissions test, Keller did as well. And so it was that he landed at the University of Vermont in medical school.

The initial thought at Vermont was to become a pediatrician. "I like playing with kids," Keller said. "I seemed to function at that level." But first Keller had to endure the six- to eight-week rotations studying various specialties. It became, more or less, a process of elimination.

He rotated through geriatrics, internal medicine, family practice and gynecology. He worked in a lockup ward, where employees needed identification to gain entry and patients had to be approved to leave. Finally, Keller rotated through pediatric surgery and his future was decided. He enjoyed the fast pace and minimal time sitting behind a desk. It seemed a good fit for his short attention span. Whereas some students would do a surgery rotation and cross it off their list, Keller was not bothered by the gore. During gross anatomy, he was always enthusiastic about dissecting the cadavers. Keller's father winced at the idea.

"Medicine grossed him out. He'd never want to hear about anything I did after I went to med school. He'd turn green."

Keller stayed at Vermont for his six years of residency and tacked on a year for a trauma critical care fellowship. That was an addition to his curriculum vitae that made Keller stand out to some extent. A pediatric surgery fellowship at Cardinal Glennon followed. Keller was taking his new knowledge of trauma care to a city where it could be put to good use. He just had no idea to what extent.

"Because I'd done trauma critical care and had more experience in trauma, it became natural to try to be a trauma director somewhere," he said. "When I was finishing at Glennon, they had a position, and Ellen didn't want to leave. I liked working at Glennon a lot, so I stayed on there."

By the early 2000s, Keller had become a well-paid — by most folks' standards — surgeon. But not a lot about his life was going to change. He became known as the guy who was apt to show up at the hospital wearing cargo shorts, a T-shirt and a baseball cap when he received a call. His pursuit of material rewards was minimal.

"He always wanted a Jeep, and two weeks after he got the job at Glennon he went out and bought a Jeep," Ellen said. "That was his splurge. Two weeks later he was saying, 'I don't need this.' He says he really just wants a fixed-up microbus, and he really does."

Keller keeps a collection of what he calls "happy vans" sitting on the desk in his office. "This is the one I want right here," he told me, pointing to a Volkswagen Samba. "I would take it in any color, although I don't really like yellow."

When he finally decided to stop driving the Jeep, handing it down to his oldest son, he opted for a Mini Cooper. That was about 16 years after he dove into trauma at Cardinal Glennon -- not a decision he would regret, but one that eventually pushed him to the edge. The increasing number of gun injuries led he and Ellen to develop an anti-gun stance that took root and grew stronger when they had children. Still, he always has been willing to treat kids injured by guns.

It fits the catcher-fullback piece of his personality. It's the part of Keller that doesn't mind getting in the trenches, in the messy and bloody battle against trauma, and plugging away until he has used every trick in his arsenal to get a patient out of the trauma bay or OR.

"He's one of those underdog kind of guys," Ellen said. "He's going to work hard but doesn't want to be in the spotlight. For the most part, you're slugging it out. He's more of a slogger. There is some sort of satisfaction in it."

There must be, or Keller never would have left Cardinal Glennon and its relatively high rate of gunshot trauma cases in

2007 for a hospital he knew would have considerably more. When he made the move in 2007, he did so with a solid reputation and a handful of trinkets for his new office, where he prefers to spend as little time as possible. He took a Superman figure presented by Glennon nurses to represent the nonstop work he had done in his final year. He took a Penn Quaker bobblehead and an empty Ivy League beer can from an antique store in Connecticut. There is a driftwood sculpture created by his son Ben with scraps from the Atlantic Ocean, and a Count Chocula bobblehead. He added a stuffed frog, which was a gag gift after being told he sounded like a frog. And there's a Smurf doll from a former patient, who arrived at the hospital virtually blue in the face, like a Smurf, he had told her.

Keller has been said to have the disposition of Winnie the Pooh's similarly blue friend Eeyore, the demeanor of a basset hound and the look of a nutty professor. His words are often minimal, as reflected by the many one-word email answers he sent me in response to what he considered overly wordy questions.

He prefers not to do interviews and expresses disdain for speaking in front of crowds. Yet, he does the latter with frequency. When Diana Kraus became trauma department manager, she persuaded him to talk to various groups, sometimes in small, rural towns that were hours from St. Louis.

"It didn't matter if there were only four or five people," she said. "He would go and bitch about it the entire time but do a fabulous job."

Even in his comfort zone in the hospital, Keller often plays a subdued role as he makes his rounds.

"He won't even go into a patient's room by himself," trauma nurse Mary Alice McCubbins said. "He'll come in the room with me but say, 'You go first.' He is a genius. I wouldn't say he's socially awkward, but he's so shy. He's under-spoken but he knows. He likes someone else to do that part."

There's nothing that quiets Keller more than an injury involving a gun that ends badly. Ellen has seen it in their home, the way he shuts down. It's the part of the job that has most impacted his worldview and even shaped the way he raises his kids. In a house without guns.

Dispatches From Keller

Most of the surgeries performed at St. Louis Children's Hospital are scheduled well in advance, allowing everyone involved to be prepared for what they will encounter in the operating room. The equipment is ready and waiting for the surgeon and nurses. Roles are not in dispute. Keller has cases scheduled most days he works. However, gun injuries are haphazard. Statistics show that they occur more frequently on certain days in certain months during general time frames. But I could have lived at the hospital for a week and witnessed the removal of an appendix most days but never seen a GSW. Hospital staff pinpointed weekend nights as having a higher likelihood of gunplay that leads to shootings. Still, on many late Friday and Saturday nights at the hospital, the halls of the emergency department are relatively peaceful and quiet.

A look at data from recent years showed that expecting GSWs to arrive on Fridays and Saturdays wasn't necessarily the best plan. In 2008, one of the high-water years, Sundays generated more GSWs than Fridays and Saturdays combined. In 2009, Thursdays were second only to Saturdays. And in 2011, the hospital was just as likely to see a GSW on a weekday as on the weekend. Although summer months tend to have the highest seasonal impact, the hospital saw 11 GSWs in April 2014, making it the busiest month during a year that would see considerable community outrage following the Michael Brown shooting in August.

The city of St. Louis has a curfew for juveniles from 11:59 p.m. to 5 a.m. on Fridays and Saturdays and 11 p.m. to 5 a.m. all other days. A study concluded by SLCH in 2015 showed that 54 percent of GSWs suffered by children 16 and under occurred between 6 p.m. and midnight, and only 17 percent were during curfew hours.

Gun injuries do not necessarily follow consistent patterns in relation to time of day or time of year. The widespread availability of guns creates myriad ways for children and teens to become part of the story at any time.

Keller agreed to send me a text message when he received notice that a GSW was en route to the hospital. In theory, that provided the opportunity to get to SLCH, meet a hospital official and attempt to gain consent from the family to watch the medical team at work. The seriousness of a case was revealed by the level of the trauma activation. Each case is identified in the initial electronic notification with one of three designations: trauma stat, which involves the most serious of injuries, likely requiring a trip to the OR; trauma minor, which might be an injury of the extremities; and trauma consult, which is a minor injury, possibly a graze. Keller's ability to text when he was the surgeon on call was more difficult than if one of his co-workers was on the case. His dispatches included the basics, often when the patient was already in the trauma bay.

Sept. 14, 9:35 p.m.	Sept. 17, 10:24 p.m.
GSW chest now	GSW 1 yr old
Bernabe on call	Now
	Not sure who is on
Sept. 18, 9:05 p.m.	Sept. 26, 11:50 p.m.
GSW	GSW x 2 EU
3 yr old in EU	I'm on call
Dillon on call	

Sept. 27, 3:56 a.m. Air rifle injury Taking to OR	Oct. 14, 4:30 p.m. GSW head Dillon on
Oct. 25, 12:48 p.m. GSW in EU Bernabe on call	Oct 25, 2:42 p.m. 2nd GSW in EU now
Oct. 25, 6:04 p.m. 3rd GSW just came to EU	Nov. 2, 12:07 a.m. GSW Saito on call
Nov. 11, 4:26 p.m. GSW in EU now	Dec. 8, 8:01 p.m. GSW 15 minutes Vogel on call
Dec. 17, 5:18 p.m. GSW EU now	Dec. 21, 3:29 a.m. GSW transfer in 1 hr Bernabe on call

It is not uncommon for the emergency room to receive no more than five minutes of advance notice that a GSW is en route. When Keller is on call, he is allowed 15 minutes to reach the ER after receiving notification. If he's at home, it's a 6 1/2-mile, 12-minute drive if conditions are perfect. Always in the back of his mind is the one time he was stopped for speeding on the way to a call. It doesn't help that construction of a new hospital wing created traffic congestion for more than a year.

The availability of five surgeons to rotate nights on call from 2012 to 2016 created a manageable balance of cases. But GSWs sometimes come in clusters. Once a surgeon takes a patient to surgery, the backup surgeon has to be alerted. Multiple shootings in a night are not uncommon, and sometimes they can be anticipated. Dr. Kate Bernabe handled three on Oct. 25, 2014, between 1 and 6:30 p.m. Dr. Jackie Saito had a trifecta on March 7 and 8 of 2015 in less than 24 hours. Keller had three in one late-night barrage Sept. 26 and 27, 2014, including a trip to the OR for an air gun injury at 4 a.m.

"I would say we all hate it," he said. "We do it because we take care of kids. You go in, and there's a chance you'll be operating, and it's going to be an all-night affair. It's completely unnecessary stuff. It's not like a kid got appendicitis and couldn't help it. It's frustrating, but somebody's got to do it. It's part of the deal if you're going to be a pediatric trauma center."

The challenge of covering emergencies on a 24-hour basis increased in 2016 when two surgeons departed and another reduced her surgical duties. On nights when the GSWs come in clusters, the potential for problems increases.

Keller had another night that he had to handle four GSWs. However, they were not life-threatening injuries, and there was just enough time between each arrival to keep the proceedings from getting out of hand. The system has been oiled well enough through continual practice that it does not tend to get overwhelmed easily. Sometimes it's the repetitive absurdity of circumstances that wears on staff members, especially those who have the most contact with GSW patients.

It is when young children arrive that emotions can fray. When the GSW volume jumped 40 percent in the first three months of 2015, many of the injured were younger than 10. Some were shot in random acts of violence, some in places that should be safe spaces such as parks and front yards. One week in March 2015, when Keller was out of town, McCubbins was feeling overwhelmed after working with patients at the hospital's trauma clinic. Keller returned to find an email from McCubbins:

"Ok, this is getting ridiculous. Really? I saw a 2 yr old and 3 yr old GSW in clinic today and now another 2 yr old and 5 yr old. Goodness, when will it stop?"

I made mad dashes to the hospital on several occasions after receiving texts from Keller. The immediate goal was to arrive in time to witness what transpires from the ER to the OR. The timing and logistics were challenging. More than once, I arrived to find Keller had come and gone. I arrived without being able to contact hospital employees to serve as chaperones. One night I sat and watched an ever-changing mix of family members and friends as they awaited an update on an injured teen and intermittently argued with security personnel in the hospital's lower lobby before being asked to disperse.

At times, my observations led me outside of the hospital, into the homes and lives of those living with the aftermath of a shooting. There I saw not only the ravages of gun violence, but of gun accidents and carelessness from guns left accessible during a typical day in homes. But the wounds are the same, and the scars just as permanent, no matter the back story.

Demetri

Tina Gaston always made a point to meet the parents or guardians of her children's friends. That familiarity gave her comfort when her oldest son, Demetri, would visit another home for a play date. But she didn't know the grandfather of the boy who shot Demetri after finding a gun on his grandpa's bed in December 2012. She knew the friend to be bright, what she considered "computer smart." Nothing told her to stop Demetri the day he asked to go to the friend's house. The boy, she had concluded, seemed responsible for his age.

The day had started like most. Tina woke her 12-year-old son and had clothes waiting on his dresser. She enjoyed overseeing Demetri's wardrobe. It was all she could do to keep him from wearing the gray skinny jeans that were his favorites, the ones he would wear for days on end. He was typically first to his bus stop, and as he left the house, Tina watched him cross the street. While standing at the door, a thought crossed her mind — one that materialized out of nowhere.

"I was looking at him going across the street and thinking that it is so wrong how people hurt kids," she said. "I don't know why I was thinking that. He was the only kid out there."

After school there was a knock at the door, like so many other days when friends came around. Tina wouldn't let Demetri leave until his bedroom was clean. So, he tidied his room with the help of his friend and then convinced his mother that a couple of pages of homework could be done later. He ran out the door at 4:30.

The house Demetri was visiting was on Westmont Place in University City. It sits in a line of small brick homes in a quiet neighborhood, awnings over the front door and windows. Westmont runs behind North and South Boulevard, where Tina lived and raised three boys on her own. The house was on the next block, "right out my window," she said. The night started quietly as she waited for Demetri to return for dinner.

The days were now short and darkness had fallen. Demetri should have been home — he usually was. Tina was talking with her boyfriend about her son's tardiness, thinking about the future. "We were having this discussion, thinking that he was going to be turning 13. And if he's doing this now, what were we going to do when he was 14 and 15," she said.

That's when the police arrived. After a brief conversation, an officer drove Tina to St. Louis Children's Hospital in a police cruiser.

On Westmont Place, unknown to Tina, yellow tape surrounded a crime scene.

* * *

Dr. Fahd Ahmad had 15 seconds to gather his thoughts before entering the room where Tina was waiting. He had been coached for this situation but was about to experience the moment for the first time. Ahmad was completing the final month of his extended fellowship and already working shifts as an attending physician in the emergency department. The ER was bustling with patients waiting to be seen. But Ahmad was focused on the message he needed to deliver.

He entered the room with social worker Stephanie Whitaker. He knew he needed to be concise and avoid medical jargon that doctors often use with each other. Skip the details that would not be important, he told himself. Tina was relatively calm, and it was Ahmad's impression that she didn't know what had transpired. He needed to speak slowly but get to the point. He sat down and made eye contact.

Demetri had been shot in the head and arrived at the hospital unconscious, Ahmad told her. He wasn't breathing. His heart had stopped. Resuscitation efforts were exhausted, and the medical team was unable to get Demetri's heart to beat on its own. His injuries weren't survivable. Ahmad was stoic but gentle in his delivery. Tina sobbed.

The young doctor said he is emotional at times but does not cry easily. He walked the line between parent and professional during a mostly one-sided talk that lasted a few minutes. He then took Tina to see Demetri and left the two alone. In the days and weeks that followed, Ahmad often thought about the moment. He contemplated the balancing act between a parent's need for information and the instinct to provide compassion and emotional support. He had asked Whitaker to analyze his conversation, and she assured him he had handled the situation well under the circumstances. His concern over the subtleties of his delivery was commendable given what he knew was likely: Tina would most certainly not remember much of what was said. Months later, she had virtually no recollection of the person who delivered the news.

"If I'm in a stressful situation, I don't want to improvise everything, but you can't script a speech when you're having these discussions," Ahmad said. "You don't ever know if what you said was the right thing. But once she hears he's dead, how I delivered it gets washed out the door and the emotion of him being gone is the only thing left."

Like his talk with Tina, the sequence of events had unfolded quickly. Police responded to the scene of the shooting at 5:47 p.m. after a burglary was reported. They found Demetri lying on the floor in a room leading from the garage to the house. He was wearing a red hoodie and gray pants. There was a considerable amount of blood on the floor. Police searched the home and didn't find anyone.

Paramedics cut off most of Demetri's clothes as they prepared to get him to the hospital, about six miles away. One officer followed the ambulance. Medical personnel received only a few minutes' notice of the arrival. As often happens with the arrival of gunshot injuries, doctors and nurses might be handling routine cases of the flu or broken bones when they are forced to shift gears for the frantic arrival of a GSW. Ahmad recalled a scenario where he was tending to a child with a broken arm. He had just delivered a strong sedative when a nurse said he was needed immediately. A boy had been shot numerous times up and down his left side with a shotgun, and one pellet lodged behind his left eye, leaving him with only one eye.

As Keller made the trek from his office, Ahmad already was in the trauma bay with Demetri. The situation was clearly dire, the only hope being to resuscitate him and get him to the OR. He was losing his pulse when he was delivered by paramedics. He was losing heart motion. With compressions and medication, the medical team was able to restart his heart and regain signs of a pulse. But they faded again and again. Demetri was bleeding from his wound. Brain matter was evident.

Ahmad concluded that Demetri had lost consciousness the moment he was struck. His death was probably certain at that moment, yet resuscitation was attempted until the boy's sad fate was clear. Ahmad pronounced Demetri dead at 6:37 p.m. The officer asked that his hands be covered with paper bags. He then bagged Demetri's white, size 5 Nikes, a pair of white socks and his favorite pants and took them to the station as evidence.

As an ER physician, Ahmad has a vastly different relationship with GSW patients than the surgeons who see them in the OR, the nurses who take care of them during their stays or the social workers who might remain in contact after they leave the hospital. All of them are likely to have repeat contact with a patient. Keller might see them during rounds for days and in clinic for follow-up care. Nurses tend to their needs in the pediatric intensive care unit or during extended stays. They get to know family members and hear stories about the shootings, or in some cases about their lives and fears and dreams.

Ahmad and his fellow ER co-workers see GSW patients for a brief time. Sometimes, the shorter the better, meaning they have been evaluated quickly and moved to a room or into surgery or, better yet, sent home. Patients in these cases can be unresponsive in the trauma bay. A physician might have a brief conversation with a parent before they move to the next step of care.

"You develop a connection in your memory with these families that don't remember you," Ahmad said. "They only need me for a tiny little snapshot, but they stay with you as an ER doctor for months or years or decades."

Demetri's case is etched into Ahmad's memory. He was just beginning his career and hadn't seen many GSWs compared with the ER's long-timers or senior surgeons. Keller's recollection of the night Demetri passed through the hospital, on the other hand, offered an insight into how many he has seen over the years. When I first asked him about the case, he didn't recall his involvement. He checked his files the next day and realized he had been present for the resuscitation attempt.

The night Demetri died, Ahmad had to regroup to handle an ER full of patients. Demetri's death left him shaken, but he still had six hours remaining in his shift. He didn't have the luxury of ducking outside for a breath of air or finding a quiet place to gather his thoughts.

"Sometimes I feel as ER doctors we just move on, and I don't think that's the best way because you're still human," he said. "You have to make sure to find a way to process things internally. The next 10 patients who are already there are expecting a well-trained doctor to be on top of their game, and it doesn't matter if they're there for a stubbed toe or a gunshot wound.

"They don't know you just walked out of a room from telling a mom her child died. And I don't feel I have a right to carry that into the next room and negatively impact the care of the next 10 patients."

Ahmad took a few minutes to walk the hall and then returned to work.

* * *

Tina keeps a photo of Demetri, her great grandmother and great, great grandmother on the mantle in her home. She has difficulty processing the idea that all three have died. An overwhelming sadness makes her petite frame seem all the more fragile. Nearly a year after the shooting, she was doing her best to put up a strong front for sons Donnel and Devin, who were 4 and 8 years younger than Demetri at the time of his death. On a warm summer day in August 2013, they rode their bikes as a new puppy chased them up and down the driveway.

The three brothers used to sleep together. Tina would find them in the morning in a tangle on the bed, arms intertwined, with legs and feet poking faces. The memories of Demetri and that bedroom were overwhelming, so she moved. She put Demetri's clothes and other belongings in plastic containers and doesn't plan to get rid of them.

After the shooting, her life quickly became a perpetual battle to maintain strength for the boys. That was difficult in the face of counseling sessions and medication for depression and the constant feeling that she was nearing a breakdown.

"I don't set a goal to make it to the next day," she said. "I set a goal to make it to midnight. If I make it to midnight, I made it just one more day of dealing without my child. One more day of getting the kids off to school. One more day of smiling when I want to cry. Every hour is different. This hour I'm talking about Demetri. The next, a smell could come through and remind me of him, and then I'm crying again."

Tina dealt with the funeral, which she doesn't recall with much clarity. Then there was the move to another house in University City. She was living in a modest home and dealing with her own medical issues, including depression and heart problems in her early 30s. Finances were an issue. "I'm not rich. I'm not middle class," she said. "I'm more like what you consider on the borderline of poor." In the months following Demetri's death, she felt discomfort interacting with attorneys and other people she described as having "so much good going for them." However, she considered the impact she could have if she could muster the courage to take her son's story to the public and put another face on the dangers of guns and children.

Students at Brittany Woods Middle School, where Demetri attended sixth grade, had attempted to make a point at the Missouri State Capitol 12 years before his death. An after-school club organized a trip to Jefferson City. After a presentation by a pro-gun group, the children placed 729 pairs of shoes on the Rotunda stage to represent the deaths of Missouri residents who had died from gunfire in a single year.

Tina wasn't sure she would ever be able to take such a stand because she was so overwhelmed in dealing with her own issues. She struggled with her inability to afford a tombstone for Demetri's gravesite. She decided not to let Donnel or Devin play at friends' homes, restricting them to visits with relatives. She couldn't understand why the family of the shooter had never reached out to express condolences, apologize or send flowers.

They didn't know the Demetri that Tina knew. The boy who loved skateboarding at an early age. The boy who loved pickles and hot sauce. The boy who listened to a little rap music, a little rock 'n' roll.

Most of all, Demetri loved to turn flips. Tina had taught him, and Demetri made it a point to teach his friends in the park, at school or at the bus stop. One minute they would be talking, the next he was doing a flip. It became his calling card, the way he distinguished himself in a crowd.

"He knew if he turned a flip, everyone around would look at him in a totally different way," she said. "He knew it would distinguish him from any kid, even if they had on Jordans or had a PlayStation. It's the one thing that took him away from other things that make kids popular, and he just ran with it."

She fights to keep those images alive. But there is nothing she can do to erase the final moments with her son. After talking to

Ahmad in a small conference room, she was escorted to the trauma bay. Demetri's body had been cleaned, his wounds dressed. As she turned the corner, Tina collapsed and nearly fainted upon seeing her naked, lifeless child. "That was the most traumatic thing," she said. "Seeing my son clothed and alive that afternoon and then seeing him naked and dead."

* * *

"Practically certain." Those two words can stand between St. Louis County Assistant District Attorney Kathi Alizadeh and her ability to prosecute cases that fit Demetri's scenario. Missouri does not have a specific safe-storage law. If adults are to be charged in cases where children find guns that lead to a shooting, it must be done under the state's child endangerment statutes, which state that a person commits endangering when he or she "knowingly acts in a manner that creates a substantial risk." Courts interpret that to mean a shooting with such a gun must have been "practically certain."

It is incumbent upon the prosecutor to prove that access to a gun would make it practically certain that a shooting would occur. That becomes the problem. There is a high burden of proof because the potential for a gun to be discharged is not enough.

The case in University City was presented to Alizadeh, who had an abundance of factors to consider. The grandfather, who lived at the residence where the shooting occurred, said he normally locked his gun in a safe. But due to some recent burglaries in the area, he had been sleeping with the gun under his pillow. On this particular day, he left for work in a hurry, and the gun was not returned to the safe. It goes without saying that an untold number of firearms are left unsecured in homes around the country every day — homes where children live and are unattended in the hours after school. Therein lies Alizadeh's plight.

"We get cases that come in where children get a hold of guns. A lot of times I have to look at the facts and scenario to see if it's practically certain they were going to get a hold of the gun and harm themselves," she said. "The vast majority of the cases we get are not practically certain. If you leave a gun out and a toddler gets a hold of it, it might be different. But an older child knows exactly what he's doing. When the grandfather left the gun in the bed, I asked myself if it was practically certain the grandson would take the gun and shoot that kid. I would have to say no."

That is the simplest way to summarize the case, which involved a considerable number of twists and turns, including a story that changed considerably over time.

Alizadeh previously had handled a case where a 15-year-old broke into a locked drawer to access his grandfather's gun. Because an attempt was made to store the firearm safely, no charges could be brought. She had seen scenarios where younger children essentially built scaffolding to climb in an attempt to reach guns. Even then, she said, "I can't say harm is practically certain."

Sometimes, however, a situation will present itself that leads to charges even though a gun never was discharged. Alizadeh's office decided to press felony endangerment charges in one such case. A young girl, who was suicidal, was given a loaded gun by a male adult and encouraged to use it. She didn't, but he was charged.

Studies show that even when parents believe guns are hidden, children find ways to get them in their hands. A 2006 study published in the Archives of Pediatrics and Adolescent Medicine revealed that 73 percent of children younger than 10 knew where their parents stored guns in the house, and 36 percent admitted they had handled those guns.

Attempts have been made through the years to toughen Missouri's laws. In 1990, a St. Louis County councilwoman introduced and then withdrew a bill that would have required firearms be locked and stored to keep them from children. She withdrew because of a state law that restricted gun laws made by local governments. In 1994, a bill was introduced attempting to make it a crime to store a loaded gun that could be accessed by children 14 or younger. A pediatric plastic surgeon at Cardinal Glennon in St. Louis told the Senate Judiciary Committee that he supported the bill after his hospital handled more than 20 gunshot wounds in children under the age of 10 the previous year. Those attempts came at a point when GSWs were escalating dramatically. In 1990, Missouri saw 78 deaths from guns among children under the age of 18. The number jumped to 128 in 1992, according to the St. Louis Post-Dispatch. In 2002, Missouri state Senator Joan Bray, from University City in the St. Louis metropolitan area, introduced a gun-storage bill that never got out of committee.

More recently, Missouri state Representative Mike Colona filed a bill in 2012 to require gun owners to either use locks or store firearms in a locked safe. Violations would have been punishable with a year in prison and a $1,000 fine. Months later, state Senator Maria Chappelle-Nadal, from University City, introduced legislation to create the offense of negligent storage of a firearm. She wanted to hold parents or guardians responsible if someone under the age of 18 took a gun to school, committed a crime with such a gun or killed or injured someone while handling such a gun. Parents also would have been required to inform their schools or school districts if they owned guns. None became law. Thus, the child endangerment law is the only tool Alizadeh and others have to prosecute. She has few cases cross her desk and estimated seeing no more than one per year in nearly two decades on the job. Only a handful have resulted in charges. It is unusual in St. Louis County for an adult to be held responsible for creating easy access to firearms by children.

In January 2015, three children found a gun in their grandmother's home in a suburb of St. Louis. A 6-year-old boy subsequently was shot in the leg while his grandma was in the shower. Cheryle Spaeth was charged and pleaded guilty to endangering the welfare of a child, which is a Class A misdemeanor. She was given a suspended imposition of sentence and two years of probation. As part of her penalty, she was restricted from having guns in her home.

In Demetri's case, the grandfather was not charged. The young shooter faced a charge of murder two in juvenile court. During the process, Tina didn't hear a word from the grandfather. The boy mustered a bit better: "I'm sorry Miss Tina," he said in court one day.

"I thought the system was out to help people who are victims, but sometimes it doesn't work that way," Tina said. "Sometimes you can become the victim all over again. It doesn't just stop with burying your child. You're the victim every time. You prosecuted a 12-year-old but let the grandpa go, knowing he was the reason the boy had the gun."

Demetri's case had numerous problems that may have played into Alizadeh's decision. The "practically certain" clause was only one consideration. Revisiting the details of the case, Alizadeh recalled the discrepancies in the shooter's story and questions they created in her mind.

The boy originally had called 911 and reported that he had shot a burglar in his home. The victim was not originally reported as being a friend or a child. The shooter also had claimed he didn't realize Demetri had followed him to his house. He later provided a different version of the story. He said that when he realized he was pointing a gun at Demetri, not a burglar, the two laughed and the gun discharged accidentally. The investigation revealed traces of Demetri's blood inside the barrel of the gun, indicating he was shot at close range. The coroner concluded in the final report that Demetri's death was a homicide.

"This was, in my opinion, really a very tough call," Alizadeh said. "In my mind, there was some question whether the kid intentionally shot his friend. Sometimes I have nothing other than my own gut. I thought there was a real question whether the kid did it intentionally or if it was the accident he made it look like."

Police departments are not required to send cases to Alizadeh's office. If a child is harmed in a shooting, the case can be hotlined to the children's division of the Missouri Department of Social Services, which does not apply for warrants. Alizadeh sometimes learns of those cases. She also considers charges in cases she hears as a member of the St. Louis County fatality review panel. Sometimes she has to consider charges in the case of suicides in homes where the parents had guns.

Access to guns in the home remains a major issue. According to the national firearms survey of 2015, there were 4.6 million children living in homes in the United States with at least one loaded and unlocked gun. Only 11 states have laws related to locking devices, and some of those states are among the lowest nationally in suicides. Laws that seek to hold gun owners responsible for shootings exist in 27 states, according to the Giffords Law Center to Prevent Gun Violence, but many allow adults to avoid prosecution due to loose wording, such as in Missouri.

"Personally," Alizadeh said, "I wish there were stricter laws."

Accidents Happen

Three sets of eyes were glued to a TV screen showing the St. Louis Blues playing the Nashville Predators. No one else in the restaurant cared because we were in Chicago, where the Blues are not necessarily welcome among hockey fans. But in this party of five, three were Blues fanatics. So Keller, Dr. Pam Choi, a resident physician at St. Louis Children's Hospital, and social worker Bobbi Williams were wedged into a booth, shoulder to shoulder, in self-induced hockey trances, noshing on deep-dish pizza and sipping beer.

Without averting his eyes from the action, Keller interrupted the hockey small talk to ask Choi about her presentation the next day at the national meeting of the Pediatric Trauma Society. This would be the first conference for the fledgling organization, which represents a tiny piece of the world of pediatric medicine. The audience would include many heavy hitters in the world of trauma care. Choi was not among them.

"Are you ready?" Keller asked without receiving a response.

His message was brief and reassuring. Being nervous would be a waste of energy because her topic wasn't controversial — not when presented to a room full of pediatric medicine practitioners. With this audience, Keller told Choi, she would be preaching to the choir.

The presentation would summarize a study Choi spearheaded looking at GSWs at SLCH over a five-year period. The title: "A single-center retrospective review of gun violence in the pediatric population." The research was limited to patients 16 and younger. The age limit was agreed upon because it matched the official cutoff for pediatric facilities in the state of Missouri.

Choi researched the basic costs of having these patients in the hospital, the circumstances surrounding each case, the demographics and outcomes. Keller believed she had information that would surprise their peers, even with an audience that knows the problem well. There was one particular statistic he considered critical to the results, and he had asked Choi to emphasize that number in her presentation. It didn't have anything to do with the number of patients who ended up in surgery or how many needed chest tubes or any other medical procedure that might apply to GSW cases.

The results weren't groundbreaking but provided a reminder that kids and guns continued to be a lethal combination. Children's hospitals in Columbus, Ohio, and Detroit were scheduled to present similar studies at the conference. Their GSW numbers for a 10-year period were roughly the same as what SLCH saw in five years.

As the pizza disappeared, the game ended and the Blues won. Choi's eyes never left the screen.

* * *

The Pediatric Trauma Society is a young organization. That's peculiar, perhaps, given that gun trauma kills more kids than any disease. Yet, the pool of pediatric surgeons specifically trained in trauma is quite small. Most who deal with gunshot wounds, automobile accidents and all-terrain vehicle crashes learned about trauma care in medical school or through short rotations during surgery fellowships. Otherwise, their on-the-job training can be left to chance, and many receive limited exposure to gun injuries.

Many who had emphasized trauma were in Chicago for the PTS conference. A majority had crossed paths through the years, especially during their formative stages of medical training. That was the case for Keller and Dr. David Mooney, a St. Louis native who is trauma director at Boston Children's Hospital.

Keller was a resident and two years behind Mooney when they met at the University of Vermont in Burlington. The college town is not exactly a hotbed for trauma, especially gunshot injuries. Keller saw one GSW during his time there, which spanned 1986 to 1996 as a graduate student, surgical intern and surgical resident. A man was cleaning his rifle when it discharged. The victim passed out after realizing he'd blown a hole in his arm. He woke up the next day to find his dog licking the wound. But despite the lack of GSWs, Burlington has a reputation for producing pediatric trauma surgeons thanks largely to one man.

Dr. John Davis served in World War II and the Korean War, working in a Mobile Army Surgical Unit. His research led to new methods for treating trauma patients. His friendship with Richard Hornberger helped shape a small part of his legacy. The two served in Korea, and Hornberger later became an author, writing under the name Richard Hooker. He is famous for his book "MASH," which became a movie and TV series. It became an urban legend in Burlington that Davis had provided partial inspiration for the character "Hawkeye" Pierce.

Davis eventually became chair of surgery at the University of Vermont and was editor of the Journal of Trauma, based in Burlington, the latter for for 19 years. He downplayed the Hawkeye story, but it persisted until his death in 2012.

"He collected all these trauma guys, these Vietnam vets and Korean vets, all into trauma," Mooney said. "A lot of his people went into trauma. A lot of residents who went there, like me, looked around and wondered who they wanted to be like. The trauma guys were the cool guys."

Davis had fallen ill and no longer was involved in surgery when Keller became a surgical intern. However, residents would present cases to him every Tuesday afternoon at his home. Despite working at a hospital where trauma was scant, Davis had a significant impact on a small field.

Along with Keller and Mooney, the University of Vermont produced Dr. Anthony DeRoss, who became director of trauma at Rainbow Babies and Children's Hospital in Cleveland, and Dr. Anthony Sartorelli, a pediatric surgeon with an emphasis on trauma at Vermont Children's Hospital. Despite his trauma background, Mooney does not see the volume of GSWs that Keller sees. In Boston, he sees a handful each year.

But he understands the landscape, having been raised in University City, which borders some rough areas in St. Louis and St. Louis County. Mooney feels a kinship with the area where he was raised. It's where his brother still works and where he shot that brother in the leg with a pellet gun while targeting frogs in a pond. It's where a classmate was shot and killed when Mooney was in medical school at Saint Louis University. Armed with a rifle, his friend confronted a burglar but was overpowered and the firearm was taken from his hands. Mooney's friend was killed with his own gun.

Mooney claimed there is not a single area in Boston where he would be afraid to drive or walk. He feels differently about his hometown. He recalled driving on Grand Boulevard, a major north-south artery that cuts through the Saint Louis University campus, passes Powell Symphony Hall and slices through the north portion of the city.

"I'm going through the heart of the north side, and I was freaking petrified to drive in the daylight," Mooney said. "The level of poverty is almost like people are like zombies with burned-out buildings right on Grand. I was thinking, 'I should not be driving down this road.'"

St. Louis is divided into six police districts, but residents are more apt to refer to areas by neighborhood names. There are dozens in the city: the Central West End, The Ville, Lewis Place, Kingsway West and East, Hamilton Heights, Penrose, Mark Twain, Academy. The portion of Grand that Mooney mentioned cuts through Vandeventer, JeffVanderLou, The Greater Ville, Hyde Park and College Hill. Grand is home to world-class theater and musical performances, but also has known great despair. In April 2015, a man was found dead in his car on Grand in the middle of the afternoon after the vehicle was riddled with more than a dozen shots from an assault rifle. Several months earlier, a man was found dead in the middle of Grand after being shot in the early evening near the Grand Center Arts District.

There is no denying that St. Louis has a gun and homicide problem. From 2010-2017, there were 1,228 homicides and 15,971 gun-related aggravated assaults. The farther north, the higher the statistics. Roughly half of the homicides since 2010 have occurred in the northern police districts.

These are the neighborhoods that produce many of the GSWs that end up at St. Louis Children's Hospital.

* * *

The trip to Chicago began when Keller drove a rented Chevy Suburban to the entrance at SLCH. Why fly to Chicago when you can put everyone in a large SUV, make the drive in five hours and save a little money? Along for the drive were doctors who had repaired hundreds of bodies injured by bullets. But there was nothing pretentious about this group, just blue jeans and snacks and random trivia questions to kill the time.

As it began to snow near Bloomington, Illinois, Keller took charge with a familiar topic. "What is the theme song from 'M*A*S*H'?" "Where is Hawkeye Pierce's hometown?" It wasn't until talking to Mooney the following day that I understood the preoccupation with "M*A*S*H."

Two days of meetings followed, mostly presentations from hospital representatives of varying stripes — surgeons, nurses, anesthesiologists, trauma managers. A converted ballroom was packed when Choi stepped forward, the crown of her head peeking over the podium as she lowered the microphone. Three gaudy chandeliers dangled overhead, and dozens of smaller ones lined the halls on the surrounding second level. It was a lavish scene for discussions of brutal, bloody injuries these people would encounter when they returned to work.

Speaking in a low and confident voice, Choi introduced her topic and proceeded directly to the point.

"Gun violence remains a significant public health concern in the pediatric population," she said, launching her eight-minute talk.

Classifying guns as a public health issue is not a universally accepted tenet. The National Rifle Association, for one, does not approve of lumping guns into the realm of public health. The NRA doesn't want doctors talking to patients about firearms in the home. In 2014, the organization fought against the confirmation of Vivek Murthy as surgeon general. The NRA didn't care for his belief that guns pose a public health threat, that doctors should have the right to discuss safety, and that federal funding should be available for such research. Choi, however, used terminology that is widely – although certainly not universally — accepted by those in the room. She discussed her methodology and steps taken by the hospital to reduce the number of gunshot victims. SLCH has distributed gun locks, instituted an intervention program and participated in gun-safety forums.

She cited a figure of 255 pediatric gunshot victims during the study's five-year period. That number would be considerably higher if victims 17 and older had been included. But it still elicited a reaction from the crowd, especially when compared with the 295 GSWs at Nationwide Children's Hospital in Columbus and 303 at Children's Hospital of Michigan in Detroit over a span of 10 years.

"When we examined the gun victim patient population as a whole, we found that the average age was 13, and patients were mostly male and African-American," Choi told her audience. "Overall, mortality was 5 percent, and 11.4 percent required a PICU admission, while 16.8 percent required operative intervention."

Then she hit on what Keller felt was her most significant discovery.

"Additionally, a third of admissions were the result of accidental injury," she said, her laser pointer highlighting the statistic projected on the screen. "Over time, we found that there is an overall decrease in total gun-related admissions. Mortality remained low while there is a slight decrease in recidivism. However, the number of victims from accidental gunshots remained stable. When we further examined this accidental population, we found there was a male predominance; however, victims tended to be younger, and there was a more equal racial distribution. The majority of incidents happen in the home."

The GSW incidents in the study were 32.5 percent accidental with 41.9 percent occurring in the home. Analyzing only the accidental GSWs, 82.1 percent happened in the home, and 50.2 percent were of the most serious variety. The injuries were 42.2 percent self-inflicted — although rarely suicide attempts — while 22.8 percent were the result of being shot by a friend and 15.7 percent by a sibling.

These numbers were critical to Keller because they showed that within the pediatric population many children were getting their hands on guns and hurting themselves or others. He believes it is information that contradicts arguments made by pro-gun crowd and NRA, which has backed legislation to keep pediatricians from talking to families about guns in the home.

"She nailed it," Keller said.

When Choi ended her talk, conference attendees formed a line for questions and comments. The line was a significant factor in how Keller judged the impact of her work. Some doctors had questions, others simply wanted to address the issue of guns and the subject's handling by the medical community. Dr. Carlos Flores from Children's Hospital of Central California stepped forward to voice an idea that other speakers repeated: "I think we lack courage. I think we lack courage because the cultural demographics are such a political hot button that we're afraid to address those."

It is the type of reaction that Keller relishes.

"I wanted to see the line at the podium," he said. "I knew it would get everybody up and riled. They weren't asking questions as much as they were using this as a rallying cry."

As conference attendees lined up to comment, Keller received a supportive text message from Dr. Mike Nance, director of the pediatric trauma program at The Children's Hospital of Philadelphia. Keller and Nance met when they were training at Penn. Nance's career had delved deeply into childhood injuries, including research on pediatric trauma, with a heavy emphasis on firearm injuries. His hospital does not see nearly the number of GSWs as SLCH, but Nance is passionate about the issue. While many of the medical personnel at the conference might have different perspectives on guns, Nance believed there was a common core belief.

"They may have dissenting views about gun control stuff but not dissenting views about the impact on kids," he said. "To a man, they would suggest that we need to figure out how to keep kids out of the mix."

Nance is a bigwig in the trauma world. His father was a longtime surgeon at Charity Hospital in New Orleans. Mike went to medical school at Louisiana State University and saw a considerable amount of trauma. Ultimately, he couldn't avoid the pull to join what he calls the "black sheep" of the pediatric surgery profession.

After the mass shooting at Sandy Hook Elementary School in 2012, Nance found himself at the forefront of a new policy statement for the American Pediatric Surgical Association (APSA). The group wanted to update its policy, which hadn't been changed since 1998 in the wake of the Columbine shootings. Because of the potentially toxic nature of the issue, the APSA board of governors decided to alter the process. The new statement was to be vetted, and then voted on, by the entire organization instead of being recommended in committee and approved by the board. So, the position paper was posted on the association's website for all members to review. Then the statement was debated at the group's national meeting. Some members reacted adversely, suggesting it was a political issue, not medical. When the vote was held, the updated statement passed with overwhelming support.

"The medical profession has a unique view that legislators don't see," Nance said. "They're not in the trauma bay. They're not talking to grieving mothers. We have an unbelievably unique and powerful perspective. We should feel an obligation to share that perspective so they understand."

Among its nine recommendations, the APSA said that firearm injuries and deaths should be addressed as a public health issue; supported universal background checks; urged an end to limitations on funding for firearms injury research; supported the limitation of access to high-capacity magazines, and supported efforts to institute more child-access prevention laws.

When Nance's own hospital decided to respond to the Sandy Hook shootings, he wasn't as pleased. He was left out of the process. The result was what he considered a tepid statement.

"They're worried about offending the conservatives," he said. "They think we'll become a political target of the NRA if we take a stand."

* * *

After the conference in Chicago, Cardinal Glennon was asked to add its GSW data to the SLCH study to create an even broader, citywide overview. When the results were compiled, the report was touted as one of the largest of its kind. Previous studies did not include the number of shootings that were handled by the two hospitals. In slightly more than five years, 398 children ages 16 and younger were treated at the two St. Louis hospitals, which are the only Level 1 pediatric trauma centers in an area that includes eastern Missouri and a large portion of eastern and southern Illinois. Two Level 1 trauma centers in Colorado completed a similar study with 129 gun-related injuries recorded over nine years. A University of Miami study included 740 GSW patients in a 20-year period. The University of Alabama-Birmingham reported 194 GSWs in 10 years.

One SLCH statistic Keller was interested to compare to Cardinal Glennon was the percentage of accidental shootings. The hospitals' findings in this area were similar. In his mind, the most significant discovery was that 31.2 percent of GSWs 16 and younger were the result of accidents. They were kids getting shot in their homes either by their own hands or those of a friend or family member. The patients who were shot accidentally averaged age 11.

Data from the Centers for Disease Control and Prevention showed that from 2010 to 2016, there were 19,565 injuries from unintentional shootings in the 0 to 19 age group as well as 828 deaths in the United States. Reports produced by several organizations, including The New York Times and Moms Demand Action for Gun Sense in America, have shown that the number of reported unintentional shootings is much lower than what actually occurs.

"Most accidental shootings occurred within the home, a place where children should be safe," the SLCH-Cardinal Glennon report said. It continued, "This suggests that interventions aimed at gun safety within the home and directed toward families would most benefit younger patients."

The St. Louis study also showed that GSWs came from 94

ZIP codes in Missouri and Illinois, spanning the city, suburbs and rural areas. Of the patients in the study, 50 percent suffered the most severe level of trauma with injuries to the head or torso, 17.3 percent needed immediate surgery and 5 percent died.

Trevin

Trevin Gamble was running down a hospital corridor while being chased by a nurse with a needle. It was his first memory after being shot. The image remains clear years later.

But Trevin knows it never could have happened because he has been in a wheelchair since waking up confused, surrounded by family. The day he arrived at the hospital, a temporary shortage of oxygen traveling to his brain caused a crippling of his muscles, his vision and speech. But he was alive. Family and medical personnel were thrilled and surprised when his eyes opened. Many thought they never would.

Although he couldn't see or speak during those first days of consciousness, Trevin recognized voices in the room. He remembered the people he heard talking but had no idea what was happening or where he was. In a short time, though, he was able to communicate. He spent several months at Ranken Jordan Pediatric Bridge Hospital in St. Louis County while preparing to return home for a life that would be much different than what he previously knew.

When I visited seven years after the shooting, Trevin was spending considerable time in his bedroom in a two-flat in north St. Louis. He lived with his mother in the renovated building, the latest of many residences since his near-death experience. The building next door was condemned. Trevin was in eighth grade when he was shot. He returned to school for a short time but eventually dropped out. His diabetic mother was unemployed.

"She can't get a job because she has to be here with me," he said.

They were living month to month, relying on Medicaid to help with Trevin's bills. He had returned to SLCH once after the shooting to have gallstones removed. He didn't recognize or remember any of the staff members who had saved his life.

He talked of finding a therapist who could help him make more significant progress. He dreamed of walking and living on his own and of taking classes or getting a job. But his ability to make a living, like that of so many other shooting victims, had been thwarted. Possibly forever.

Ted Miller, Ph.D., a researcher at the Pacific Institute for Research and Evaluation, has studied economic impact related to GSWs nationally based on a large array of factors: costs for medical treatment, mental health, employers, police, adjudication, insurance claims and quality of life, among others. Using SLCH statistics for 2014 and 2015, he estimated the cost for patients seen at the hospital came to $76 million. When those losses are concentrated in a relatively small area, the impact can resonate throughout the community.

Trevin doesn't think in those big-picture terms because his struggle is daily. A lot of the details of the afternoon he was shot are unclear, either because he can't remember or was never told. He asked me if they cut his chest open in the emergency room and if his family was there. He seemed unaware that a large portion of his left lung had been removed. But he was aware of the dire situation he faced when some people inside the hospital suggested he would live the rest of his life in a vegetative state.

"They said they could have pulled the plug," he said. "They said they were going to see if I made it, and I made it."

Seven years later, Trevin's body was thin and frail. He weighed 90-something pounds, and his ankles had withered to the point that a hand could wrap around their circumference. His right foot was twisted outward, pointing at a 45-degree angle. He did not have full control of his arms and hands. The scar that was left from opening his chest was wide and dark and straight, following a line from the middle of his chest and around the curve of his left side, nearly reaching his back.

"That ain't never going nowhere," he said.

He told me he could tell that I have gray in my hair and could see my face, but he couldn't make out my eyes or my lips.

A nurse visited the house seven days a week to help with portions of his daily routine: getting out of bed, washing, cleaning his room, preparing food, using the restroom. Trevin could eat finger foods without help but needed the proper utensils for some meals. This is the daily existence that had to be accepted long ago.

"At first after the shooting, everybody was hurting. After a while things got normal again," he said. "Everything felt normal to me when I came home, it's just that I wasn't walking. The first couple of years I didn't really do too much. I was just in the house or going to therapy. I didn't want to do nothing, just get up out of this chair."

Trevin became accustomed to spending most of his time at home, mainly because his family didn't have transportation. He relied on prearranged transportation to take him to an exercise facility, where he worked on strength with the hope of walking again. But his transportation was sometimes unreliable. He was especially frustrated about the van not coming one day that he was scheduled to receive shots of Botox to help relax his muscles so they could function better.

Part of the normalcy of life was the knowledge that so many other relatives and friends had been impacted by similar circumstances. His aunt was shot and killed in St. Louis in the days before I visited. He knows others who have been killed or injured by guns since he was shot. The day he was targeted, Trevin was with two cousins and a friend. One cousin later died in a shooting in 2014, and the other ended up in jail. His friend also was jailed. He heard that the man who fired at him was killed in a shooting.

Life became unsettled the day Trevin was shot. "I've lived so, so, so many places," he said, "I can't even count."

Aside from his mother, Trevin spent a year living with one of his sisters. He moved in with a cousin, then his grandmother and then an aunt. He stayed with friends for periods of time. He also spent five months at a rehabilitation center in Columbia, Missouri. His life has been disrupted in countless ways.

At his latest home, Trevin's wheelchair didn't fit through his bedroom door, so he used an office chair to watch TV or play video games. He navigated the rest of the apartment with the wheelchair. He used it when he took showers and to spend time outside on a small stoop. That was usually the farthest he could reach the world outside.

After three months in his newest home, his mom wanted to find a new place to live.

"We caught 23 mice on traps," he said. "I don't like them mice. They're in my bedroom, too, but they can't get on my bed because it's up high. But they were getting on my mom's bed when it was on the floor. I don't like mice."

Corey

Surgical fellow Tammy Mirensky and I had planned for a breakfast meeting to discuss her two years at the hospital. Staff members were more available to talk in the mornings, when kids were in school and less likely to be doing some of the stupid or dangerous things that land them in the ER. But Mirensky and I had been talking for less than one minute when her pager signaled a trauma stat activation -- the most severe level of trauma -- at 8:08 a.m. At 8:11, I received a text message from Keller, alerting me to a GSW. Moments later a 17-year-old boy was wheeled inside after being shot once in the back while walking to school.

Corey (not his real name) was being placed on the bed as Mirensky approached him from the side and Keller assumed his position at the foot. As Mirensky began the primary evaluation, Keller started his routine. The patient was conscious, and his vital signs did not indicate a major, impending problem.

"How many shots did you hear," Keller asked Corey. Silence ensued. "Dude, how many shots did you hear?"

"One," came a weak response.

There were 17 staff members in the trauma bay at the peak of activity, five standing to the side with no clear, designated roles, necks craning for a view. An infant was delivered to the opposite side of the bay and was crying hysterically. Keller considered the location of Corey's wound, feared the bullet had pierced a kidney and decided he needed to find out if the teen had blood in his urine.

"We have to put a catheter in your bladder," Keller said. "It's going to be painful, but we've got to do it."

Corey was not going to avoid surgery. Keller asked for imaging that would provide two internal views -- one a lateral across Corey's abdominal wall. He instructed the OR nurse to head to the sixth floor to prepare.

None of Corey's family members had arrived. He was asked if he had eaten anything and responded that he had only brushed his teeth. At 8:30, social worker Bobbi Williams called Corey's mother. After giving her a quick summary of what had happened, she handed the phone to Mirensky.

"By the time you get here, he'll be in the OR," Mirensky said. "So, don't rush and get into an accident yourself."

The hospital's director of public safety, Terry Kowalczyk – one of many to hold this position in a brief time — roamed the hall, making sure all was calm. A St. Louis city police officer arrived. This is often the case when a shooter is on the loose. The officer was there, in part, to check on the victim's status in case homicide detectives would need to be called to the hospital.

The scene was relatively calm under the circumstances. Medical personnel who bustled about Corey worked with a sense of purpose but not with the chaotic feel of a patient whose life was in danger. Surgery is no longer an absolute when someone takes a bullet to the abdomen. Imaging has improved to the point that many injuries can be managed without operations. In fact, bullets are often left inside patients. But in this case, Keller was unable to determine what organs or vessels had been hit. Corey was taken to the sixth floor for a laparotomy, a procedure that allows for exploration of the abdominal cavity.

For most of the 20th century, gunshot wounds to this area of the body were generally believed to require surgery. But in the last two decades, that convention has been challenged, leading to a decrease in laparotomies. Surgeons often found in the past that the procedure was unnecessary after it was completed. And, of course, avoiding a trip to the operating room saves money for the patient and ultimately for the hospital that may not ever collect.

An extensive study by Johns Hopkins Hospital revealed that, indeed, many surgeries for abdominal penetrating injuries are not necessary. But it's not that simple. Because the research also showed that if the wrong patients are selected for observation, the results can be deadly.

"Managing gunshot and stab wounds without exploratory surgery prevents complications and keeps 80 percent of patients from getting operations that end up being unnecessary," according to surgeon Adil H. Haider, the study's senior author. "But not every hospital should pursue this course because if physicians make a mistake, the patient pays."

Haider's team looked at records from the national trauma data bank covering 2002 to 2008. The more than 25,000 patients with GSWs and stab wounds were of all ages. Of those patients, 22 percent of people with gunshot wounds did not undergo immediate surgery. However, of that group, 21 percent ultimately needed a trip to the OR to take care of complications.

Keller didn't feel that Corey could wait. At 8:47 a.m., he began his ride to the OR.

* * *

Robert Plant's voice soared overhead as Led Zeppelin's "Whole Lotta Love" greeted Keller in the operating room.

Corey was sprawled across the surgical table 90 minutes after a bullet stopped him from reaching school. Two units of blood were on hand if needed. The music seemed louder than might be comfortable for conversation in a restaurant while nurses, an anesthesiologist and Keller prepared for what figured to be a standard laparotomy.

By the time Keller was done scrubbing, sheets were draped over the boy's legs and upper body. His abdomen was left exposed. Mirensky hovered over the small patch of skin with an electrocautery device in her right hand and calmly announced the start of surgery: "Making incision." Within seconds, smoke swirled from Corey's belly, the smell of burning flesh sharing the air with The Animals' "House of the Rising Sun."

Keller's first order of business was to control the bleeding. That allowed him a clearer view of what had transpired. He looked for holes in the intestines and applied a couple of quick stitches. At that point, he was able to analyze the bullet's path. Two X-rays were displayed electronically on a screen with an "X" marking the entrance wound. The bullet's position was obvious. It rested near Corey's spine, and 10 minutes after the initial incision Keller found it, noting that it seemed to have pierced a kidney. The Rolling Stones' "Tumbling Dice" churned in the background.

A nurse was asked to call for a security officer, who would be needed when the bullet was retrieved. Keller plucked the bullet from the anterior abdominal wall and dropped it in a plastic specimen cup. The cup was placed into a baggie and passed from one nurse to another. The names of each person to handle the bullet, cup and bag were recorded for the officer, who stored the contents until they could be picked up by the police as evidence.

Corey was walking to his St. Louis city high school in September 2013 when he was shot a block from campus. The incident was not regarded as a school shooting, of which there had been dozens since the mass murder at a Newtown, Connecticut, elementary school on Dec. 14, 2012. In fact, despite occurring two blocks from campus, the school didn't bother to go on lockdown

Corey was a senior and had plans to attend a culinary college. In fact, the night before he was shot, a representative from a school in Louisville, Kentucky, visited his home to discuss the details of his possible enrollment later in the year. To get there, he would need to graduate from a city school that suffers from a high dropout rate.

"What school does the kid go to?" Keller asked during the early minutes of surgery.

"Hard knocks," responded nurse Rachel Aurelia, who was nine months pregnant but digging in for two hours at the table as scrub nurse.

"You guys are brutal," Keller said without halting his work.

The music had stopped playing, and the most audible sound became the constant suck, suck, sucking of blood from the opening in Corey's midsection. Keller asked for someone to lower the table. A nurse noticed that the handle on an overhead light was smeared with blood and about to knock Keller in the head. The handle was replaced. The surgery had been ongoing for 30 minutes when Keller made a discovery.

"I think it went through his renal vein," he said.

The renal veins connect the kidneys to the inferior vena cava, carrying purified blood.

"Can you get me Jeff Lowell or somebody from transplant?" Keller asked. "I just want to run something by him. The kid has a renal vein injury. The question is, does he want to try to repair it, re-implant it, or does he look at it and say it's not fixable and then we'll take out the kidney?"

* * *

Some GSWs can be monitored and treated without surgery because of the ability of certain organs to withstand the impact of a bullet and heal themselves. In some cases, it is better left inside the body rather than taking a chance with an invasive procedure that could make matters worse. The question that has to be answered is whether other injuries were incurred or if the damage is isolated to a specific organ.

Keller learned long ago that the type of bullet and firearm can determine the severity or nature of the injury. Ballistics became part of the equation while he was at Penn. If a bullet wobbles or tumbles, it can spread the transfer of energy. Hunting rifles will produce more kinetic energy from a greater distance than handguns. Additionally, the tissue that is damaged inside the body will react differently depending on the density. If a bone is struck, it can fragment and produce further injuries. However, sometimes a bullet striking a bone is fortuitous because the energy is dissipated.

Advances in imaging combined with other factors have given surgeons more tools to decide whether an injury requires surgery. But it is often far from cut and dried.

"That's always been the argument," Keller said. "Is it unnecessary to do an operation to explore and find out nothing is injured? Or is it good to operate and find out nothing is injured? People interpret it different ways."

Studies on the topic have been conducted for decades. Although the frequency of a nonoperative approach has increased, the acceptance of that practice is not universal and remains in question because many patients who do not initially have surgery end up needing a trip to the OR. A survey of trauma surgeons in four countries, including the United States, conducted by the University of Aberdeen in the United Kingdom in 2013 reflected the continuing conundrum. Of the 183 surgeons who replied, 57 percent said they practiced what is known as selective nonoperative management of abdominal gun wounds. Surgeons who had completed trauma fellowships, such as Keller, and who worked at facilities that see more than 50 abdominal GSWs annually, were more likely to avoid surgery when it was thought unnecessary.

A reduction in surgery, it cannot be denied, also has financial ramifications for the hospital. Dr. Brad Warner acknowledged there is a push to be more cost-effective. So, with evidence pointing to a need for fewer OR trips for GSWs, the trend has its benefits. Warner, however, wasn't saying that decisions are ever made based on finances.

"Many involved in gunshots are not card-carrying insurance holders," Warner said. "It consumes a lot of time and resources, and reimbursement is very low. That has an impact on your overall division. If revenue is lower, you can't pay people as well or you have fewer and fewer people. Or, you pay them well and they're on call every second or third night. Finances have an impact. You have to offset it with other things you do."

Still, surgeons confronted with trauma cases typically aren't thinking of finances. And some situations are almost automatic in regard to a trip to the OR. When a victim is shot in the "box," the odds of surgery increase. The "box" covers the area above the belly button, below the suprasternal notch in the throat and between the nipples. Of the people shot in that area, 40 percent arrive at the hospital unstable and in need of surgery. And although 60 percent are stable, half of those patients will need surgery. Corey fell into that category. Using imaging and knowledge gained from vast experience, Keller was able to develop an idea about what injuries had been inflicted. One of the basic guidelines that Keller follows is to determine the bullet's path. One day, he pulled a stuffed animal – a gift from a patient — off the shelf in his office to demonstrate how he uses entry and exit wounds to visualize the internal path, lining up point A with point B. It is simplistic but helpful in gauging what organs were likely to have been damaged. The younger and smaller the child, the more organs that could be impacted.

If a patient is stable, the time required to get results from a CT scan can be worthwhile. This imaging technique can pinpoint the location of injuries and is often the difference between a patient going to the OR and being admitted for observation. Sometimes only an X-ray is necessary. That was the case with Corey because further imaging was not required to determine that the bullet had entered his abdomen. A form of scan known as a CT angiogram is used to look at blood vessels. Corey did not undergo that test, but Keller later said the bullet missed the inferior vena cava by maybe one millimeter. The vena cava is one of the body's major arteries and returns blood to the heart. It can be repaired but also can lead to death if punctured.

Finding the bullet sometimes can prove to be a challenge, more so if it ends up somewhere far from where it entered. If a bullet settles in someone's stomach, it may migrate to the digestive system by the time surgery starts. In that case, Keller is likely to let the patient pass the chunk of metal instead of trying to find it in the intestines. Bullets also have been known to remain in a blood vessel and travel, similar to a pulmonary embolism.

Because the internal organs vary in texture, they react to bullet wounds in different ways. Damaged blood vessels need immediate attention due to the danger of exsanguination, which is blood loss severe enough to cause death. They often can be fixed with stitches, but options such as artificial veins and artery patches are available. Bullets will pass directly through many organs, such as intestines, the esophagus and sometimes lungs. Lung injuries occasionally can be treated with a drainage tube that allows the lung to re-expand. However, there are times when a lung leaks so much air that surgery is required to halt the leak. Lungs are one organ where a bullet might be left if it is too dangerous to attempt removal. The liver falls into the same category but is denser. If it is determined that the bullet struck only the liver, that patient might be observed.

"If you think you're going to get a bullet out of the center of the liver, it's not going to happen," Keller said.

However, because it is full of vessels and bile ducts, a bleeding liver often requires surgery. Stomach injuries have to be repaired. An injured pancreas typically requires surgery and is a nuisance because it has a texture like cottage cheese. The spleen, like the liver, can be stitched although a bullet is unlikely to strike only the spleen. Kidneys also can retain a bullet and might be left alone if determined to be the only injury. However, 60 percent of GSWs involving a kidney require surgery.

"Sometimes if it's real bad — if there's major bleeding and the patient is barely alive — I've gone into it thinking, 'I can only do good on this patient. There's nothing I can do that's going to make it any worse. And no one will point a finger at me if I don't get this guy out of here,'" Keller said. "I've had a couple like that. Once when I operated, I had a resident tell me a few weeks later the only reason the patient made it was that I was there. I had the trauma training to do it and thought about it differently than others, and my approach was different."

* * *

Forty-seven minutes into surgery and 10 minutes after he first asked, Keller waited for Lowell and his expertise. In the meantime, with assistance from surgery fellow Dr. Annie Brady, Keller had freed Corey's intestines from his body, and they literally sat outside of his abdomen on his belly.

"Mom is in the waiting room," said nurse Heather Denochick. "Is there anything I can tell her just yet?"

"He has an injury to his kidney. He's stable. Trying to figure out if this kidney injury is repairable," Keller said.

"I'll just say you're still working on it," she said.

"When's Jeff coming?" Keller turned his head to look at the clock. It was 10 a.m. One question needed to be answered. And in deciding about the kidney, Corey's race had to be considered because African-Americans have a higher incidence of renal failure later in life. Thus, the steps that might be taken to reconstruct the vein or save the kidney would be more aggressive in this case than some others. However, if the main renal vein was badly damaged, the kidney might still need to be removed.

At Keller's request, a slush machine was wheeled into the OR at 10:04 in the event that surgical slush, which cools organs and reduces their need for oxygen, was needed during the removal of the kidney. Keller checked the clock again at 10:08, and Lowell walked into the room two minutes later.

"Gunshot to the back, 17 years old," Keller told him. "He's got an injury at the mid-portion of the right renal vein. He also has a couple of holes in his colon. No spillage. He's got a left kidney by palpation. Somehow it managed to miss his IVC."

Keller completed his summary as Lowell gazed at the X-ray.

"That's old school," he said. "He's probably the only person in the whole hospital who hasn't had a CT scan today. ... It's so quiet in here."

"I was trying to listen to music," Keller said.

They turned their attention back to Corey's kidney. Lowell requested a Bookwalter, a retractor that helps to expose areas of the abdomen. As the minutes ticked away, a discovery was made. A larger vein going to the kidney, which was determined to be the main vein, was found. Corey, it turned out, had an uncommon anatomical feature, and it was his good fortune.

"We won't need the Bookwalter," Lowell said.

Just like that, disaster was averted. The conversation turned to football.

One hour and 40 minutes after surgery began, Corey's abdomen was closed. Keller walked to a dry-erase board and attempted to illustrate with a marker what had transpired. Corey had two holes in his bowel, which were stitched. The bullet caught a portion of his liver, where Keller inserted a drain. The liver would heal itself. The scenario involving the right kidney was not what had been feared.

Two days later, Corey rested in his room. He was under blackout status, meaning his name would not appear in the hospital's registry and his presence at the hospital could not be divulged by any employees. He recalled he was walking to school with a friend when a group of kids challenged him to fight. When someone pulled a gun, he turned to run and was struck.

It turned out that the three suspects were students and former students at Corey's school. He and his friend saw them emerge from a walkway. One suspect began yelling at Corey, who walked toward the three to see what they wanted. One of the men was upset about a previous dispute with Corey's cousin. Another of the suspects removed a gun from his waistband, according to three witnesses. He handed the gun to another person, and as Corey attempted to flee he was shot in the back.

The witnesses at the scene identified the participants in the shooting individually from photos and lineups. The police visited Corey in the hospital. He was in stable condition at the time but couldn't move well and struggled to speak. Medication he was given after surgery left him drifting in and out of consciousness. When he was alert enough, he was able to identify all three attackers. Corey attempted to circle the photos of the people he identified. His mother signed off as a witness.

"I knew them," Corey said. "I'm not really afraid because I know what they're capable of and what they're not. I've got a lot of friends who have been shot. I've seen it."

This was clearly mere bravado from a tough-talking teen because it was apparent the shooter was capable of murder. So, those words did nothing to appease Corey's mother, who had feared her son was dead or paralyzed when she heard he was shot in the back. Police officers had paid her a visit during the surgery to provide an update. Corey's mother was ready to enforce restrictions: No more walking to school. No staying after school. No walking in the neighborhood with headphones over his ears.

"I know he's probably scared as I am because he knows they're looking for him," she said. "The kid who shot him has been in jail a couple of times. He's only 17 years old. How long can he run on the streets? You can't stay running forever when you're only a kid."

The person identified as the shooter was arrested and admitted his involvement, in an interview with the police. He and his friends had stopped at a vacant house that morning and obtained a gun. Community guns are known to sit in waiting, their locations known to residents who want them.

"We were all playing with it in the vacant house," the shooter told the police. "We left there and then got into it with some dudes. I was just trying to scare the dudes. I tried to shoot a bird that was above their heads."

That story didn't quite hold up. Later, the shooter pleaded guilty to charges of armed criminal action and first-degree assault.

Helping Hands

Rachel Aurelia had only two hours of experience observing in an operating room when she was hired as a scrub technician at SLCH. She was simultaneously working her way through nursing school. The OR, in essence, became her second classroom where she would attempt to fit the skills learned at school into real-life scenarios. But Aurelia discovered that the systems and methods of the hospital were like nothing she was being taught. She quickly came to dislike the hospital work because the nursing skills she was learning in school did not seem to apply to the OR. She didn't understand the flow of the OR and was overwhelmed by many of the cases. She vowed to find another job as soon as possible.

Aurelia applied elsewhere with regularity until a longtime employee advised her to give the job one year. By that time, she was told, she would have learned the ropes and would love the work. Thirteen years later, Aurelia was patrolling the sixth floor and walking the halls as a veteran nurse with the self-assurance of a veteran surgeon. In fact, she had been working at SLCH longer and had seen more gunshot wounds than almost all of the hospital's operating staff.

The 15 operating rooms are the domain of Aurelia and her fellow OR nurses. It's no different at any hospital: surgeons get the glory, but the nurses keep things running smoothly. Aurelia and her team are masters of the OR logistics of what needs to be done, by whom, where and with what equipment. Surgeons don't just lean on them, they rely on their expertise and ability to be tossed into a wide range of roles. In surgery scenarios, they can work as scrub nurses or circulating nurses. When nurses are "scrubbed in," they set up necessary equipment for an operation and assist the surgeon directly. Circulating nurses work outside of the sterile area and assist with other tasks.

In her early days, Aurelia worked 24-hour shifts, an arrangement that exposed her to an abundance of GSWs. She was forced to learn on the job and found herself working regularly as a scrub nurse, directly linked to life-and-death propositions.

"I had to get used to the amount of blood and trying to keep up with that," Aurelia said. "Knowing you're behind is not a good feeling. The kid is bleeding out in front of you and you see it's dripping off the table, but you're doing everything you can. It's getting used to that mindset. You keep going and hope you can catch up because it can be a lot of blood.

"I've only had a couple where they open the abdomen and blood starts pouring out. You see it rolling out of the patient and down the table. It's quite surreal."

The sudden nature of cases is not as jarring on the sixth floor as it is in the emergency room. In most cases, there is time to get the proper equipment arranged and for personnel to be in place by the time the patient has gone through the trauma bay and been carted upstairs. The system became better organized when it became a requirement for an OR nurse to report to the ER when a trauma case is en route to the hospital. But there are still surprises.

Nurses receive notification on pagers along with surgeons and others who are vital to cases. That initial bulletin can provide the information that dictates the degree of urgency.

Sometimes the information is wrong, unclear or incomplete. One night Aurelia and her fellow nurses received notice of a gunshot victim arriving with a thigh injury. No major organs were involved, based on information they received. But when the boy arrived for surgery, nurses discovered a bullet had punctured the femoral artery. The patient was bleeding out. There was no pulse and the trip to the OR came quickly. The surgical team needed access to a table that was not readily available. An angiogram was required to view the severed artery. A swap had to be made on the fly. The standard surgical table was rolled away, replaced by a specialty table.

It was the type of case that tests every aspect of the team's preparedness and ability to adjust on the fly. It also was a case that makes gunshot cases different and, in some ways, more challenging than the scheduled procedures that often dominate a day.

"I've had a lot of exposure with gunshots," she said. "I've had situations where a kid is rolling into the room, and I literally have a knife blade on a knife handle and nothing more because I haven't had the time to get anything else ready. Adrenaline is pumping and your hands are shaking a little bit. I love the adrenaline rush part of it. It's kind of sick but I do."

In her 13 years at the hospital, Aurelia witnessed a physical transformation of the OR. An entire constellation of upgrades and new equipment were assembled, many with the aim of better accommodating child gunshot victims. Speed and efficiency are the drivers of the changes. Even subtle adjustments to equipment and their juxtapositions seek to shave off seconds in how fast a patient can be treated.

The ORs are better prepared for cases with high volumes of blood, thanks to larger suction canisters that can hold 20 liters. Nurses previously had to take time during surgery to switch containers as they filled, an unnecessary and cumbersome task. An argon beam, which uses argon gas to stop heavy bleeding, is at the ready. A designated trauma OR in Room 11 includes a trauma-specific table that allows for imaging of patients. The table is marked with orange tape as a reminder that it should never be moved. Nurses set up Room 11 every night to avoid last-second scrambling for equipment for the next case.

SLCH also began using custom-made trauma packs. They are included in the standard Room 11 set-up, eliminating the need to gather pieces of equipment individually, as was done when Aurelia started. The basic package includes gowns, ties, sponges, drapes, knife blades and Bovies, which are used to control bleeding. The basic packs are stocked with about 100 items. The remaining equipment that might be required is stored in the Central Processing Department on the sixth floor.

The push for efficiency and speed has worked. The use of trauma packs alone has greatly reduced the number of items needed to be fetched from the CPD during an operation. Other packs made specifically for chest injuries, vascular injuries or transplants are pulled as needed. It's a much more organized and tidy system than what previous generations of nurses had to navigate.

Once in the OR, nurses must account for the equipment from the packs as surgery is ongoing. Toward the end of an operation, two nurses will count the blood-soaked sponges that have been tossed in the trash to assure that none have been forgotten inside the patient. It's easier said than done. The sponges come in a variety of sizes from 4 inches x 4 inches to 18 x 18. During surgery, they can be tucked under an organ or packed in a cavity, sometimes becoming hard to detect after becoming saturated. For that reason, the sponges are made with X-ray bands that help determine the whereabouts if one is sealed inside a patient.

"I did a chest trauma with Dillon," Aurelia recalled. "We got to the end. His chest incision was not that big. By the time we finished counting he had already closed the first level, and we were off by one. I had to tell him. Surprisingly he didn't scream at me. He opened it up and there it was. It's a little embarrassing to tuck tail and say you're missing one."

Earning the confidence of individual surgeons is a process unto itself. Each one brings a different personality to the OR, as well as varying degrees of patience to deal with mistakes or curveballs or a piece of equipment that might be delivered slower than expected.

OR nurse Heather Denochick had to clear that hurdle with Dillon and remembers clearly the night she succeeded during a trauma case. She was juggling three tasks at once — holding a retractor, suctioning and attempting to pass an instrument — when a fellow assisting with the surgery barked at the more experienced Denochick. Dillon intervened on her behalf.

"That was the day me and him clicked, and I proved myself to him," she said. "It was chaotic and I was doing three different things at once. You have to gain their trust, some more than others. It's just a matter of proving you do know what you're doing. They have to know they don't have to wait for you to think about what you're doing. It was one of those things where I felt, 'He's got my back.'"

* * *

Rania Allen was working as a respiratory therapist in 1979 when her 4-year-old son died. She briefly considered leaving the medical field. When Allen decided to remain at SLCH, she requested a job that would reduce or eliminate contact with patients. She became a perfusion assistant in the OR and then earned two degrees. Allen has been working in the OR as a nurse for more than two decades.

Patients come and go every day. But from her perspective, the element of human contact has been largely eliminated. When children arrive in the OR, they are usually under anesthesia; it's the same when they leave. And for many, that makes the OR experience less emotional than it might otherwise become. The patients usually cannot talk. They are draped except for the area of the incision and the work being done. Contact with parents or loved ones often is not necessary.

"I used to get so involved with the families and patients," Allen said. "After my son died, I didn't want that anymore. I used to take them to the zoo on my day off. I had teenagers, and after they'd go off to college, they'd come back and we'd go out. I had to get away from all of that. I want to see them when they are asleep, and when they leave me they are still asleep, and I don't have to see all the families and all of the hurt and pain."

She endured that pain with her son. And she's seen more of it in recent years as a resident of Ferguson in the wake of the Michael Brown shooting. Her home is a minute drive from the hospital in a town that has received an unnecessarily bad reputation in light of the turmoil that followed the incident and subsequent unrest. It was bolstered during the 2016 presidential campaign of Donald Trump, who erroneously called Ferguson one of the most dangerous cities in the country, if not the world.

It's where Allen raised her family and remains rooted. She and her husband live a couple of blocks from the pizza joint that was destroyed in the wake of the grand jury decision not to bring charges against the officer who shot Brown. The furniture store is gone along with the resale shop, where Allen bought a set of bar stools, partly out of need but also to support the local business owners. It was an unassuming community until the developments of 2014.

Allen and her husband own guns and take the responsibility seriously. One day, when emotions were still high in the wake of events in Ferguson, they went to a county government office to tend to some paperwork to make sure all of their gun records were up to date. They found themselves waiting with a young man, who had just been released from jail. He was accompanied by a woman. The man had been cited for selling T-shirts without a permit. The woman was complaining about having been maced during the protests. Their anger was palpable.

"They were talking about how it was their time now and Ferguson might as well get used to it," Allen said. "He started talking crazy and getting loud and belligerent. My husband was squeezing my hand, but I couldn't hold back anymore. The man was from Kansas City. I told him I live in Ferguson and raised a family there."

Then came the message:

"I told him, 'If you come on my property talking about tearing it up, I'm going to have something for you.'"

Having seen enough of the destruction that people can do to each other and themselves while on the job, she draws the line when it comes to her home and her community.

Despite the attempt to distance herself from patients, Allen can't avoid occasional contact with family members when she has to discuss an impending case or provide updates on surgery. She has needed to calm distraught or angry parents. In those instances, she is able to summon her experience and a calming tone to handle potentially explosive moments. She dealt with one impassioned father who was directing his anger, and probably some fear, at a surgeon who was about to operate on the man's son. The anger was expressed in the form of a threat. Allen suggested that threatening a surgeon who had his son's life in his hands was not the best approach.

And there are still times she is unable to avoid conversations with patients who are conscious and alert before going into surgery. Such was the case one night after an older teen had been shot. He was heading to the OR but still demanding his cell phone so that he could make a call to arrange for revenge on the shooter.

"Those are the types of thing you deal with, and you have to be diverse enough to say, 'A cell phone is not what you need right now. What you need is this bullet out of your ass.'"

Police officers also are known to challenge the authority of personnel on the sixth floor. They are sometimes aggressive in their pursuit of information from or about a patient while nurses prepare for surgery. The circulating nurse usually decides whether an officer is allowed to be in the OR. Allen offers them one of two spots: outside the room or in the waiting area.

"Sometimes police are really ignorant," she said. "My thing is that I don't care what someone did on the street. When he comes in here, I'm going to treat him. When we get done, we'll turn him back over to you. Some try to come back because they say he's in their custody. That's my domain back there. You cannot come back. They're asleep and not going to do any harm to anyone. They're not going anywhere."

Treating GSW patients who were also involved in illegal activity — possibly shooting or killing someone — is not uncommon. It's an issue that hospital personnel have to process on their own terms.

That became a topic in St. Louis in October 2016, when an 18-year-old shot and killed a St. Louis County police officer. The teen was shot by another officer but survived and was treated at another hospital. He was charged with first-degree murder and armed criminal action. Bail was set at $1 million. All the while, he was being kept alive. It is that type of scenario that makes it preferable to many at the hospital that they not know the circumstances that led to a patient coming under their care. It is their job to keep the person alive, regardless of circumstances. Allen doesn't ask questions about patients, she just acts. Her natural instinct is to help anyone in need of care.

She was sleeping one night when her pager sounded just after midnight. A gunshot victim was arriving at the hospital. Allen called the hospital to get an update, but the person on the other end was so busy that the phone was set down with the line open. Allen could hear the chaos on the other end. Although no one spoke to her, the conversation she overheard made it clear that help was needed.

"You go into this in an altogether different mode," she said. "You just rev up and go into action and don't think about it until it's over. You don't think about the ramifications or 'I can't believe we lost all that blood' or 'I can't believe he was shot like that.' You just get into the mode of doing everything you can and thinking the patient is going to leave the OR."

* * *

Each time Mary Alice McCubbins sat on a patient's bed to chat, she knew there was a chance she would be witness to a story she didn't necessarily want to hear. It was the price she paid for her nurturing and protective side that made patients comfortable and willing to divulge information. Her title of trauma nurse practitioner couldn't begin to fully encompass the array of responsibilities McCubbins handled or the skills she possessed until her departure from the hospital. Gaining the trust of patients was a natural talent she brought to the job along with a gift of gab.

As a foster parent, she had seen children from many difficult backgrounds and with an array of needs before stepping foot in SLCH. Relating to kids came naturally. So her conversations with shooting victims often were littered with highly personal details.

"It's almost shocking how open these people are," she said. "I go in as non-threatening with them and say, 'What the heck?' and they say, 'This is what happened.' Then I have to go out of the room and pick up my chin. You'll tell anything to your priest and your doctor. Sometimes they tell me things I don't want to know."

It didn't take long for McCubbins to become known as the hospital's "trauma momma." She arrived in 2008, just in time to handle the boom years, tag-teaming with trauma social worker Bobbi Williams to build a rapport with patients. She was frequently the go-between when making rounds with Keller, whose interaction with patients has always been more professional than personal. She worked extensively with some kids when they returned to visit the trauma clinic for follow-up treatment.

McCubbins brought a wealth of medical experience that predated her days at the hospital. She spent the bulk of her career in the Navy and Air Force as a nurse, working 17 of 22 years in pediatrics. She was deployed during the Persian Gulf War from

August 1990 to March 1991 on the hospital ship USNS Mercy, a floating hospital that is 894 feet long, 106 feet wide and has an 80-bed ICU. She left the Navy in 1991, got married and ended up enlisting in the Air Force in 1993. She deployed in 1996 after the Khobar Towers bombing in Dhahran, Saudi Arabia. Over the years, she worked in California, Washington, Nebraska and Texas.

She ultimately transferred to Scott Air Force Base, which is 25 miles east of St. Louis on the Illinois side of the Mississippi River. At that time, the base was sending a large number of troops to Afghanistan and Iraq, where a huge portion of the care needed was for injured children. As a pediatric specialist, the chore of training people to aid with childhood injuries fell on her shoulders. She prepared 1,500 troops for that work and then retired from the military to take the job at SLCH.

"I always joke with my active-duty counterparts that I see more gunshot wounds as a civilian in a children's hospital than I ever did as active duty treating adults," McCubbins said.

She and her husband became foster parents upon leaving the military. Almost immediately, a family of six children with various needs was placed in their home. After the first year, the oldest boy was removed from their care because of his extreme emotional problems. McCubbins and her husband adopted the remaining three boys and two girls. They also provided care for sexually abused children. They had as many as 13 children in their house at one time. One of the boys McCubbins adopted developed a condition called neurofibromatosis, a genetic disorder that causes tumors to grow on nerve tissue. He died in 2006. Through various medical and special-needs scenarios, McCubbins developed even more knowledge about taking care of kids from all backgrounds. Despite the many challenges she encountered, she never had second thoughts about fostering children.

"I did it because I couldn't not do it," she said.

The same could be said of how she feels about patients and the many troubles they bring to the hospital.

"I try to approach patients by identifying their needs, and they may not be medical. They might come in with a gunshot wound to the hand, and they're going to heal and everything will be fine. But they can't go to school because they're unsafe. Mom is an alcoholic or dad is abusive. Those are parts that if you don't ask, you don't know. How do they get better and not fall into more violent behavior if we don't ask?

"It's made me better hopefully, and I try to look at it that way. I've seen the worst of the worst, and I've seen these kids are in places through no fault of their own. They still deserve to be taken care of as if they were the prince of China."

McCubbins became the perfect fit for a job that included a somewhat ambiguous description when she started. There was a need for a liaison between the hospital's services and the patient, specifically in the intensive care unit. McCubbins improvised, and she worked herself into the daily routine and prayed that she would survive her first evaluation. She survived the first evaluation and every one thereafter.

McCubbins viewed every child who came to SLCH as one of her own. She referred to "my two babies," who were shot in the same incident as toddlers. There was a boy who was shot and paralyzed when he was 14. Another boy ended up in jail after being shot and returned a few times for follow-up care.

"One of my kids," she called him. "Every time he comes in, he looks me up and says, 'I messed up.' But at least he doesn't look at me and say, 'You didn't help me.'"

The assortment of patients with gun injuries she helped ranged from completely innocent children to teens under house arrest and constrained with ankle bracelets. She worked with alleged criminals in shackles who went from her care to the hands of the police. Some returned for follow-up treatment in shackles. Attempting to work within the boundaries of hospital and police protocols, she sometimes sought to have the restraints removed for the short time these patients were with her. All the while, a police escort was either in the treatment room or just outside the door.

"I probably push the limit a little, but I try to be safe and reasonable," she said. "The kids are lovely because they get out of jail for a while. The joke is that if I see them on a bus one day, they'll take care of me."

On-The-Job Training

Even amid the intense pressure of treating gunshot victims —
and sometimes specifically in those instances — Keller must
teach. Because St. Louis Children's Hospital is associated with
Washington University, and the hospital's doctors are all employees of the university, it is a teaching hospital. It's the type of
place where a parent might be taken aback by the youthful appearance of the person who arrives to check on a child in the ER.
Those who are in training are part of an eclectic mix of caregivers, ranging from the relatively uninitiated to ready-for-OR
surgeons.

Regardless of their status as medical students, residents or
fellows, all learn the ropes at SLCH, presumably at their level of
readiness. The cast is constantly changing. For Keller, that
means a trainee who arrives in the trauma bay might be someone he's never previously seen. Keller could be standing bedside
and not have much insight into the skill level of someone who is
present to lend a hand.

"We have so many people down there, and some days there
may be a trainee from Barnes and I don't know them," he said.
"You could be in there one day and be 'physician right.' If I
didn't know you, I'd tell you to put a chest tube in."

The measure of a person's ability to handle a penetrating
trauma in many cases can be traced to the stops made along the
way. Hang around the SLCH trauma bay long enough, and

you'll get experience treating gun injuries. However, at many hospitals, a trainee might not see any. For Dr. Kate Bernabe, exposure to gunshot wounds was sparse before she arrived in St. Louis to begin a fellowship in 2008. She attended medical school in Miami, completed her surgery residency in New Orleans and was a surgery fellow in Cincinnati. But little of that prepared her for what was to come. Learning the necessary demeanor for and treatment of penetrating wounds was a matter of on-the-job training, all of which was absolutely necessary if she was going to continue her career in St. Louis. Often, the best and most thorough education does not come through schooling but by being thrown into the middle of cases to sink or swim.

In Bernabe's case, the horrendous nature of some injuries wasn't what was overwhelming in those early days. She's a surgeon who is proud to proclaim her ability to handle the mess of it all. "I don't mind blood. I don't mind brain matter. I don't mind fatty tissues from the abdomen coming out."

Slight of stature with straight black hair and a no-nonsense approach, Bernabe possesses the tough exterior of a seasoned veteran. There is nothing about her disposition that reveals a lack of confidence or the chance of becoming unnerved. That wasn't always the case.

Bernabe attributes much of her demeanor to an upbringing she could only assume was the norm. She was raised in Jersey City, New Jersey, where she witnessed violence and drug use. Drug dealers walked the streets. There were many homeless. Her family didn't always have access to a car, so they used the bus and subway, exposing three children to all that came with them. She had relatives and friends who joined gangs. The violence of her surroundings eventually prompted Bernabe's parents to move the family to rural Florida when she was 10.

But she was re-introduced to violence upon acceptance to the University of Miami's medical school. There, she worked at Ryder Trauma Center at Jackson Memorial Hospital, one of the busiest trauma centers in the country. Bernabe lived in the Little Havana neighborhood. Driving to church, she traveled on streets that produced many of the gunshot victims the hospital treated. But Bernabe had little contact with those patients, so while she knew of the carnage, hands-on experiences were fleeting.

Medical students with whom she trained had four focuses. They inserted Foley catheters, performed femoral artery sticks, cut clothes and inserted nasogastric tubes. It was somewhat robotic work, but students became adept at their core chores. They practiced by putting IV lines into each other in the lab. But the trauma that Bernabe saw was mostly due to blunt-force injuries. As a med student, she certainly never witnessed anything as dramatic as a thoracotomy, which is an ER surgery to open a chest. Opportunities decreased further when she started her residency at Ochsner Medical Center in New Orleans.

"Exposure to trauma went down to almost nothing being at a private hospital," she said. "We were about four miles from Charity and University hospitals. Ochsner is private, so everybody had insurance. We weren't even seeing indigent patients because you couldn't walk to Ochsner because it was so far from the city. To meet our trauma numbers, we had to go to a trauma hospital."

That meant traveling to Mobile, Alabama, and hospitals in eastern Texas for rotations that lasted four to six weeks. As a surgery resident, Bernabe was required to work 20 trauma cases, although there was no differentiation between penetrating and blunt trauma. Thus, she could have met her requirement without ever having seen a gunshot patient. The standard two rotations for trauma, however, were not enough for Bernabe to participate in 20 cases. So, she had to do a third.

"I wasn't at a level where I had to make major decisions," she said. "As long as the head surgeon told me what to do, I did it. Not until my fourth year did I see a case of a bullet through the abdomen as the chief handling it. When I came to St. Louis I was not thrilled, and I was very nervous."

* * *

By the time surgery fellow Dr. Derek Wakeman arrived in the trauma bay, the initial evaluation of an injured 8-year-old boy had been completed. An ER resident had taken charge of the case when the patient arrived at 8:30 p.m. with leg and chest wounds. The patient was clearly in respiratory distress, breathing rapidly and unable to speak. With a trip to the OR possible, Wakeman was well within the boundaries to assume control from the resident as treatment proceeded. It's a transition of power that is not unusual but one that can require a delicate yet forceful presence. In this case, the treatment and transition were merely a practice run.

The patient was a mannequin that had been prepared to resemble a gunshot victim. Just enough red dye had been applied to replicate blood. Dollops of makeup created the look of lesions. Clothes had been cut to correspond with the location of bullet wounds. For a handful of residents and fellows, the 8-year-old's future was in their hands in a simulation that could result in the loss of his artificial life. When young physicians arrive with little or no experience in GSW cases, simulations are one way to give them a chance to work through the steps and face the pressure, albeit manufactured.

Wakeman's arrival for the simulation was purposely delayed. While it is important to practice the decision-making that is involved in treatment, communication plays a vital role as well. Stress between co-workers can increase the tension, thus the dynamics of the transition need to be smooth. Wakeman was told to arrive late, giving ER personnel a chance to begin an assessment and consider the next steps.

"They have control while they're alone," Wakeman said. "But for a gunshot patient, I'm going to take that over. As a surgeon, that's a little more my realm, and I see that more than they do, and the stakes are higher. On consults, I'm fine letting them be the lead and even some trauma stats. But a gunshot wound is a little different. I know the ER resident chief didn't feel she had as much of a role once I got there. She felt like she was the third wheel. But in my mind, for that type of injury, I'm going to take that over."

One of the main goals of the simulation was to test how individuals would react to the changing dynamics and accept roles as the case moved from one phase to another. In the background, Keller and Bernabe observed along with ER attending physician Bo Kennedy. The mannequin had been programmed so that the vital signs would worsen with time if proper and timely steps were not taken.

The plan designed by Dr. Charlie Eldridge, who was running the simulation center at the time, was extensive, especially considering that the simulation would last no more than 20 minutes. The boy, dubbed Tommy, was assigned initial vital signs with a heart rate of 135, a score of 15 on the Glasgow Coma Scale, and a blood pressure of 94/60. He had 1-centimeter circular entry and exit wounds on his torso and left thigh. The list of learning objectives for the brief exercise was lengthy:

1. Identify problems with communication within a medical team.
2. Identify problems with communication between medical teams.
3. Improve transition of care between medical providers.
4. Identify a critically injured patient.
5. Identify causes of compromise to breathing.
6. Treat causes of breathing compromise.
7. Discuss when RSI (rapid sequence intubation) is indicated with penetrating chest trauma.
8. Discuss risk of RSI in penetrating trauma pre and post chest tube placement.
9. Identify complications of RSI prior to chest tube placement.
10. Understand how to place a chest tube.
11. Identify causes of compromise to circulation.
12. When to give blood products, MTP (massive transfusion protocol), permissive hypotension.
13. Identify which patients should go to the OR immediately.
14. Understand how long it takes to get the OR operational after hours.
15. Understand number of bullet holes should be an even number to number of shots, or else there is a retained bullet.
16. Understand where thoracic cavity stops and abdominal cavity starts.
17. Understand the treatment of orthopedic trauma in the setting of complicated chest/abdominal trauma.
18. Understand how to evaluate vascular trauma.
19. Understand how to identify compartment syndrome.
20. Understand how to treat open orthopedic trauma.

It had been decided to hold the simulation in the trauma bay, forcing the use of a less intricate mannequin. The model in the simulation center on the fifth floor could not be moved because of its intricate wiring and connectivity. It replicates many more human traits and offers considerably more options for training. But Keller and others agreed that using the trauma bay was more important. For one thing, when simulations are held upstairs, the necessary medical tools already are waiting for the participants. Thus, not only is there no need to find things in the stress of the moment, but the presence of equipment gives everyone involved a hint about what will unfold. In the trauma bay, everything that is required must be found at a moment's notice.

"We try to throw in things that happen that make a resuscitation more difficult to allow people to think about how they're going to manage those scenarios," Keller said. "In the ER, if you realize the mannequin has a collapsed lung and someone says they need the chest tube tray, a nurse has to find it and it becomes more of a benefit to them."

As Wakeman took control of the case, Karin Jackson ran through the ER halls, screaming loud enough to generate glances from those not participating in the drill. "Where's room 15? Where's my baby?" she yelled.

Jackson burst through the door into the presence of a dozen caregivers and onlookers. A member of the hospital's staff of actors, Jackson participates in simulations regularly. She played the role of the victim's mother. Because parents are allowed in the trauma bay during actual cases, their presence must be accounted for to prevent them from becoming a distraction or impediment. Second-year fellow Dr. Katie Leonard intercepted Jackson, who had made a beeline for the bed.

Leonard grabbed Jackson by the hand, guiding her to the side but within visual distance of the work being performed. Jackson had worked herself to a level of outward distress.

"What do you mean they can't find all the bullet wounds?" she shouted.

Leonard explained that Tommy had been shot in the chest. As he began to deteriorate, Leonard relayed that he was having trouble breathing and needed a breathing tube. Jackson became emotional. Tears formed in her eyes and rolled down her cheeks. She can visualize a simulation as a real-life scene easier than most.

A mother of four, Jackson had seen all of her children require treatment at SLCH, some with their lives hanging in the balance. Her daughter Caitlin had endured seven heart surgeries. Other medical scares produced a lasting tie between her family and the hospital. That is a requirement for the actors who participate in simulations. They must have a child or grandchild who has been treated at SLCH. Jackson draws on her range of experiences when she's in the moment.

"The doctors are treating it real, so it feels real to me," she said. "I was probably a little more hysterical in this one than I tend to be in others because it really did feel real."

Actors are given artistic license to portray what they think would be a possible parental reaction given the circumstances. Jackson once contemplated what a parent's reaction would be if a child appeared to be on the brink of death in the trauma bay. So in the midst of a simulation, she ran to a trash can and vomited. Another actor went into hysterics, threw herself on the floor and simulated a fainting spell.

"That was highly entertaining," Eldridge said. "She collapsed in the middle of the bay, and people were like, 'Is this for real or what?'"

As the simulation unfolded, the staff determined that Tommy could wiggle his toes, squeeze fingers and follow basic commands with some limitations due to pain. There was a delay in getting a chest tube inserted so Wakeman handled the task. It was a minor glitch he later realized could have been avoided if he had delegated the work more efficiently. This was the time to work out the kinks.

"We got to the point we were going to intubate and were asking for medications," Wakeman said. "I asked for certain meds based on what I do. But there probably would have been a better set of medications for that patient. Perhaps I should have asked my ER colleagues what they would give because they do that more than I do."

Ultimately, it was determined this was a nonoperative case. Tommy would be admitted and observed. Eldridge could begin planning for the next simulation. The chance to practice gunshot cases in this setting does not happen frequently. The hospital usually runs a half dozen major trauma simulations each year. They usually coincide with the time of year that a particular accident is most likely to occur. In the winter it might be a case of hypothermia or a house fire with carbon monoxide poisoning. Work focuses on burns and fireworks injuries around the Fourth of July. And there is always room to practice treatment for automobile and ATV accidents.

Each simulation concludes with a debriefing, in which the exercise is analyzed, and mistakes are discussed and corrected. These meetings can become emotional, especially if the mannequin dies.

* * *

One challenge when building a trauma department is that relatively few who enter pediatric surgery are interested in making trauma a long-term pursuit. Trauma cases wreak havoc on personal lives and schedules because of the amount of time that is spent on call. It's unpredictable, hectic, stressful and messy. Throw in the high volume in St. Louis, and prospective surgeons often finish their training with little enthusiasm for that area of work.

Keller realized long ago that up-and-coming surgeons do not understand the challenges. So he volunteered to give lectures at conferences held by the American Academy of Pediatrics to provide the details of a trauma surgeon's experience. It's a reality check that helps weed out those who aren't suited for the work.

"I was asked what I wanted to talk about. Since everyone who comes through says they want to be a trauma director, and I know they're all bullshitting me, I said 'How about I give a lecture on what it's like.' If they were telling the truth, then this lecture is for them. If not, it's their payback."

For those who are accepted for a residency or fellowship at SLCH, there is no choice. You learn about trauma whether you want to or not. But many end up with no interest in advancing to a job that involves treating trauma patients. Drs. Tammy Mirensky and Annie Brady had overlapping fellowships but emerged with differing views.

Mirensky wanted no part of dealing with gunshot cases when she left SLCH after two years, even though she received strong reviews from Keller and proved capable of handling GSWs without significant help from veteran surgeons. She had previously worked in New Haven, Connecticut, where there was a fair amount of gun violence but not among pediatric patients.

She didn't see many gun injuries during training in Philadelphia either. Brady, on the other hand, trained in Miami and saw a considerable number, so the barrage at SLCH was not out of the ordinary for her. She left with a willingness to work in the future at a hospital with a heavy trauma load.

In St. Louis, the two learned something about the region that they found disturbing. They discovered the gun culture was unlike anything they had experienced in other cities. Mirensky had one patient who needed surgery and requested a date that wouldn't conflict with deer hunting season. She had children who told her about the guns in their houses, including a 4-year-old who bragged about his family's collection of 70 firearms.

"The parents were there and very supportive of this," she said. "That was a shock. You have the kid with the dad sitting there dressed in camouflage."

Brady recalled a cancer patient who was having a port inserted for the purpose of receiving treatment. A request was made for the port to go on the side of the chest opposite from where the child held a rifle. One shooting victim arrived with a leg injury and explained that he was struck at a party where guns were being fired for entertainment with adults present.

"I'm from Miami and did my training there and have seen a lot of gun violence, but I was shocked when I saw what happens in St. Louis," Brady said. "In Miami, it doesn't seem there's a culture of children with guns. Here, there's a culture."

When surgeons in training get a look at the injuries and learn about the pervasive nature of guns in the community, it can lead them to the conclusion that SLCH is not a place they want to continue a career. They may learn the techniques necessary for treatment, maybe even master them through repetition. They might develop the sense of calm and creative decision-making required to guide them through cases, but the idea of dealing with the problem on a regular basis can be enough to drive them away.

Mirensky was clear as she neared the conclusion of her fellowship. She wasn't interested in hospitals with a heavy trauma load that would have her on call for such cases night after night. She was involved in many cases over two years at SLCH and earned the confidence of the staff. But she determined at some point that her personality didn't fit the model that was suited for trauma.

"We're all type A, and we like things organized and structured," she said. "I don't like the chaos of gunshots and traumas and not knowing what to expect. Some people thrive on that. I did the best I could but don't think that's where I excelled. I find it much more stressful."

Maybe it was her long-term exposure to gunshot trauma, but Brady emerged with a different perspective. She was not going to avoid a job with trauma as a major component.

"A lot of us like trauma at the beginning as residents because it's when you get to do the most," she said. "Once you've done a sufficient amount, you love it or hate it. I like the problem-solving and ability to use whatever resources you have in making quick decisions and really like the knowledge you're saving someone's life."

The perception of a pervasive gun and violence culture in St. Louis was a common thread acknowledged by many of those who learned in the system. They were students, residents and fellows who trained without previous knowledge of the city. Some came from cities or regions with an abundance of crime and shootings, but newcomers sensed something different about St. Louis.

Lola Fayanju came from the East Coast and spent her early childhood in Newark, New Jersey, which, like St. Louis, has a reputation for a high crime rate. She went to medical school at Washington University and then embarked on a lengthy residency with no inclination to take on trauma as a career pursuit. She was struck by what she witnessed in day-to-day life in the city as much as what she saw inside the hospital.

Fayanju loved trauma cases when they arrived while she was working. But like many, she quickly recognized the downside. "I have no interest in being a trauma surgeon in part because I don't want to do call throughout my career," she said. "You want to appreciate being home with your family."

She moved to a specialized area of study, focusing on outcomes and treatment disparities in patients with breast cancer. As a fellow, she won a breast cancer symposium merit award for research looking at barriers to mammography among underserved women. Her highly specialized area doesn't match the characteristics required for the field of trauma.

Still, she viewed the educational experience of working GSW cases as second to none because patients presented a vast array of unknown circumstances that tested her skills. She figured that if she learned to handle traumas, she could increase her career options. But she heard the negative side from veteran doctors and nurses, including an attending surgeon who told her that the repetitiveness would grow old, even when it came to the operating room.

Fayanju is fascinated by social implications related to GSWs and what she referred to as a "culture of violence in St. Louis." Upon moving to the city, she was struck by the number of men she saw in wheelchairs, many of whom had been paralyzed by gunshot wounds. That prompted her to contemplate the lost earning potential of families, and, in fact, entire communities.

"I think people from here can't appreciate it," she said. "But if you're from somewhere else you realize how different St. Louis is in terms of people you wouldn't think of having a gun having a gun. The level of gun ownership frightens you."

"We all come into the world five to ten pounds. I take mine home to parents who shower them with messages of love and peaceful resolution. Some are going home to a spanking in the first month. I just don't know where in the process of becoming an 18-year-old we could intervene so that those children don't grow up to think it's OK to point a gun. I don't know how we get to that point."

* * *

Bernabe handled so many gun injuries in eight years at SLCH that she is unable to remember the one that started everything. Time and volume dulled her memory. But she remembers clearly the only two gun trauma cases she handled as a resident. On the first, the attending surgeon allowed her to perform a bowel anastomosis, a procedure that connects two portions of the intestines. The second was an attempted suicide in which the patient survived a gunshot to the head. They remain vivid because they came at a time when they were completely out of the ordinary for Bernabe.

After completing her fellowship in St. Louis a few years later, it seemed Bernabe was on call when GSWs arrived more often than not. Hospital records indicated she saw a significant jump in major trauma cases compared with other surgeons. She worked upward of 100 such cases during her time at the hospital, which ended in the summer of 2016.

The first case at SLCH that stands out in her mind involved a fatality. It was a 30-year-old who was dropped at the hospital while she was a fellow. By that point, Bernabe was starting to come to grips with the standard procedures and demeanor required to make things run smoothly. However, this was a case that tested everything she had learned. An attending surgeon had not arrived when she decided it would be necessary to open the patient's chest in the trauma bay if there was going to be any chance of saving his life. This is a decision that is not taken lightly. History had proved that the procedure was not always embraced after the fact. Because no one could locate the thoracotomy tray, Bernabe had to start with a scalpel, which made the job much more difficult. When the patient couldn't be saved in the OR, the feeling of defeat was like nothing she had experienced. But she knew she had reached a turning point.

"I actually remember handling it really well," she said of the entire process. "It was my first open chest as a fellow. I was a senior fellow by then and had handled a lot. Basically after that, there wasn't anything else that I could have learned or made me more shocked."

The learning curve had been tackled, and soon the arrival of a patient who had been shot was routine. Bernabe lived in the city's Dogtown neighborhood south of Forest Park. The hospital borders the eastern side of the park. She was close enough that answering call afforded her plenty of time to make the drive with little chance of arriving late.

Bernabe discovered that work in the trauma bay and OR was not the biggest challenge. Learning the manner in which you command the team when a case arrives and gain the confidence of all participants was more significant. Fail to do so and a surgeon faces the prospect of losing control. Having worked many GSWs during her time as a fellow helped Bernabe navigate that process before she became an attending surgeon. She was given the power to act as trauma chief. As she progressed through a case, she would repeat aloud what needed to be done and then do it under the watch of a veteran surgeon.

Bernabe's naturally calm demeanor was the perfect antidote for calming a chaotic situation or soothing hostilities that might arise among those working a case. She had seen the reaction when a central line was pulled from a patient after much time and sweat was expended. She had heard harsh profanities exchanged over disagreements or mistakes. Bernabe's voice has a soothing effect, yet she became capable of persuasive force that came from being battle tested in a short period of time.

She handled so many gun trauma cases as a fellow that the ER physicians and nurses became comfortable with her style. She strived for consistency in her work so that everyone on the team knew what to expect. She toed the line between calm and bossy and communicated constantly with those involved with a patient. She learned from Keller how to remain cool under pressure but gave direction in a direct style that more closely matched the way surgeon Pat Dillon works. She accompanied Dillon on many GSW cases in the early years, a repetition that helped fine tune her skills and decision making.

Keller was always comfortable working with Bernabe as she progressed through the system. Surgeons at SLCH refer to a colleague who assists with a case as a "dance partner." Considerable experience together can result in flawless outcomes, or you can trample one another to the point of bumbling and complications.

"We didn't have to talk that much about the case because we'd done so many together," Keller said. "We could talk about anything else and get a case done. There are some who you never get to that level with. Their hands are in the way all the time."

Over time, Bernabe learned precisely how she wanted to handle the treatment of gun injuries. Her intent was to remain unemotional and avoid information about how injuries occurred. She didn't want to know if a shooting was gang-related or if a child was injured while sleeping on the living room couch. She felt that outside information could complicate the situation. Would she have reacted differently, for instance, had she known the 30-year-old had been involved in a robbery before arriving at the hospital? She simply needed the basics: Where is the wound? What are the vitals? How many shots did the patient hear?

"I go down there, I'm calm and I just have to get it done," she said. "That's how Keller is. He talks the same way every time, and I learned from him. The situation will always be different. Different people, different chaos. There's rarely any order unless it's driven by me. When I get down there, I'm running the show. I don't want anyone to get hurt or anyone's feelings to get trampled on while we're taking care of kids."

Bernabe traversed the learning curve quickly. She became adept at handling most internal injuries but always hoped that her patients did not have damage to major arteries — the massive bleeding wounds. She largely sidestepped those problems aside from the fatality in the OR, where she nearly slipped because of the large quantity of blood on the floor.

Gun trauma patients came and went, and Bernabe forgot the details of most. Some, however, did stand out. There was the girl who was shot while sleeping on her couch. During surgery, Bernabe pulled fibers from the furniture's material out of the child's body. There was the case where the bullet barely missed the aorta, somehow finding a path between the heart and a vein that could have caused the type of bleeding she dreaded. Over time, Bernabe saw patterns among the patients. A boy shot when he was 6 returned with another gunshot wound when he was 8. A teen who required surgery for his injury returned to the trauma clinic for follow-up care and introduced himself.

"He was with his girlfriend and said, 'We know you,'" Bernabe recalled. "He said I knew one of his family members. And I did remember him. It was also a gunshot but not as lucky. He's alive but a paraplegic. I took care of him a lot. But I'll tell you, I never came across a gunshot wound kiddo who was rude to me. They were always very polite."

After having her third child, Bernabe left SLCH, deciding to work part time at other hospitals. She finished her tenure in a different place than when she arrived. She started out frightened by the prospect of a GSW arriving in the trauma bay. In the end, she did more than her share to save St. Louis children caught in the gunfire.

The Bullet

While awaiting a trip to an operating room, Maurice Walker considered the places on his body where he could have been shot. He had been a moving target, and the shooter fired haphazardly, leaving the result to dumb luck. "I was glad I didn't get shot in my back," he concluded. "I would have been OK anywhere but my knee, my ankle and my back. And above my neck. Anything else would have been OK because I like to play sports."

Maurice left out a few of the more problematic locations, but he knew he was fortunate. The happy-go-lucky high school student had stopped at a friend's home two months earlier and was preparing to leave with a group that was lingering in the yard. That's when a car pulled up and a man stepped out, shooting into the crowd. Maurice slipped through a gate in an attempt to escape toward the back of the yard, but a bullet caught him in the rear end and lodged in his left hip.

Considering all of the things a bullet can do when it enters someone's body, his situation was certainly fortuitous. More often than one might think, a bullet will lodge itself without exiting. Sometimes they are removed, and sometimes surgeons determine it is better to let them remain.

Maurice's bullet seemed harmless enough the night he arrived at SLCH, chatting with medical personnel as if nothing had happened. When he complained of recurring pain after being released, the decision was made to remove it. The 15-

year-old, who weighed 225 pounds when he was shot, wanted to resume playing high school football. He had dropped to 183 pounds since the shooting. Removing the bullet would serve two purposes: Maurice's pain would subside, and a piece of evidence would be available should it be needed in court. The first time Maurice arrived to have the bullet removed, he was prepared by attendants for his trip to the OR before nurses discovered he had eaten breakfast, a no-no before surgery. He was sent home. The second time he was ready.

In the OR, two nurses were needed to roll Maurice onto his right side so that his left hip pointed toward the overhead lights. The atmosphere was casual, and chatter filled the room before a procedure that figured to take 15 minutes. There was nothing in the way of complications that might arise as Keller prepared for his second bullet removal of the morning. A handful of assistants made idle chit-chat.

"I recorded the VMAs last night," someone announced to no one in particular. "You see the Miley Cyrus thing?" came a response.

"I fast forwarded through the whole damn thing. That was just horrible."

"When I saw Mick Jagger, he had these giant bald women come on stage during 'Honky Tonk Woman,'" Keller said. "Was that much different than what she did?"

"This was nasty," came the response. "Nasty?"

"That's the only word for it."

Suddenly a nurse announced the start of the case. "This is Maurice Walker, and he is allergic to mushrooms but no allergies to medications. Removal of foreign body, left lateral buttock side for Dr. Keller. Does everybody agree?"

Knowing the exact location of the bullet, Keller made a tiny incision. At this point, it became subject to a litany of guidelines that must be followed to remain a viable piece of evidence. Keller secured the small piece of mangled metal with his fingers and placed it in a cup. It was then transferred to a biotech hazard bag by the scrub nurse and handed to circulating nurse Kim Deters. The name of each person to handle the bullet was recorded. Documentation of the chain of custody can be vital.

An officer from public safety was summoned to pick up the package. Deters documented the pick-up on a pathology sheet and typed the officer's name into a computer file. The officer then secured the contents of the bag until it could be picked up by the appropriate police agency.

In a subsequent bullet removal a few months later, the OR nurses became frustrated when public safety didn't respond to their call. And then even more frustrated when the information requested for the form exceeded what anyone had ever requested. Beyond recording the gender and race of the people who handled the bullet, security asked for birth dates. So, in the midst of stitching a patient's colon, Keller was asked to provide his date of birth for the paperwork. In that instance, Keller had to use forceps to remove the bullet, a move that is frowned upon.

"You're not supposed to touch it with pickups because if they want to do ballistics you could put a scratch on it," he said. "But sometimes you have no choice because you can't get it out. On this kid, I had to touch it a little bit to get it out. If that changes the ballistics, it changes. I can't do anything about that."

"Depending on how good the surgeon is, he could screw that up and you'd never know where the bullet came from," said Terry Kowalczyk, the hospital's public safety manager at the time. "You want to keep it as pristine as possible."

The possibility of a bullet becoming evidence is real. Dr. Bernabe vividly remembers the first time she removed one. Two police officers had arrived along with the patient, and they were not going to leave until they had at least attempted to collect some information. The officers were on the sixth floor during surgery and approached Bernabe when she was done, peppering her with questions.

How many bullets did you remove? Where was he shot? Can you identify the entrance and exit wounds? Bernabe had been warned during her fellowship of such occurrences and to be careful with answers, or not to answer at all. That's especially true of entry and exit wounds, which can be difficult to differentiate. The information can be vital to the police in determining specifics of the shooting.

"I learned on my own to have that sense of confidentiality about what should be said and how it affects the evidence and a case," Bernabe said. "I just take care of a patient and document everything in a very unbiased and factual manner. They can always go back and look at my notes."

In Maurice's case, the bullet was in good shape, unlike the one Keller had removed earlier in the day. That one had been flattened because it struck bone. Whether Maurice's bullet would be used as evidence was unknown to Keller and the OR staff, but the chain of command had been followed. Keller guessed that this projectile would not be needed. There are, however, plenty of precedents.

A murder in St. Louis in 2010 led prosecutors to request that a bullet be surgically removed from the arm of the alleged killer. It was regarded as evidence after an 18-year-old was arrested for shooting and killing a former police chief. The victim had returned fire and prosecutors sought the evidence, hoping they could prove that his bullet was in the teen's arm.

In an incident related to the Ferguson protests in 2014, a young woman was shot in the forehead. Remarkably, the bullet did not reach her brain. There were conflicting reports about how the shooting occurred with some on the scene reporting the shots came from a passing car. After the woman underwent surgery at a community hospital, the bullet vanished. Attorneys for the injured woman were first told by hospital staff that the bullet was lost and then that it was picked up by the police. The uncertainty reinforced the need for strict guidelines when handling potential evidence.

Doctors at SLCH have collected so many bullets that they decided to study three years of cases to determine outcomes. The research covered 2008 through 2010, a period in which 244 gunshot patients fell into the required criteria. Of that group, 129 had bullets that remained in their bodies after the incidents. Only 17 percent of that subset had them removed during surgery. That left 107 patients walking the streets with some type of ammunition in their bodies.

Problems that developed included chronic pain, abscesses, cellulitis and elevated lead levels. Fourteen required removal at some point. Of the possibility of an elevated lead level, the report said "presenting symptoms can be vague and the consequences significant, warranting continued surveillance in children at risk." Issues with lead were most common when bullets remained in spots where absorption was most likely such as spaces around the joints, fractures, pleural spaces or in contact with cerebrospinal fluid. An estimated 15 percent of retained bullets end up causing long-term problems that can require more aggressive treatment.

Maurice's problem was strictly one of pain, and for that he was fortunate. The gathering that led to the shooting started as a visit with close friends after a game of basketball on a warm June night. An argument started in the house and seemed to end when a group of girls left. But when Maurice and others were talking outside, the girls pulled in front of the house in one car followed by the shooter's car. The front yard became a shooting gallery and four teens, ranging in age from 13 to 17, were hit along with a 34-year-old woman. It was a night that saw 17 people shot and one stabbed in an array of incidents in St. Louis.

Maurice's grandmother rode with him in the ambulance to SLCH while his mother followed. But instead of entering the ER, his mother took time outside to gather herself. She was angry, trying to understand what circumstances could have led to another family member being shot. She prayed before walking through the metal detector and into the ER.

"I told the police I didn't know who would shoot him because he don't do nothing," she said. "All he does is play basketball, play football and sit in the house. He's not even an outside kid. When he goes out, he goes somewhere recreational. He don't smoke, he don't drink, he don't smoke no drugs. So how did my baby get shot?"

The shooting was precipitated by an argument and a fight, as many are. This time it was between the girls, who had a confrontation earlier in the day over clothing that had been borrowed and never returned. They left with the threat: "We'll be back."

When they returned, about 30 people had gathered outside a two-story apartment building. A male with dreadlocks and wearing an orange shirt stepped out of the back seat of a Dodge Magnum and began spraying gunfire randomly into the crowd. Other than Maurice, the injured included a girl who had a bullet enter and exit her left thigh, a boy who was shot in the left leg, a boy whose right inner forearm was grazed, and an adult shot in the right thigh. The injuries could have been worse. The crowd had included small children in strollers.

In the days that followed, police conducted interviews with witnesses, who were in agreement that the shooter went by the nickname "Savage." His real name was unknown. However, he was easily tracked through Facebook, where photos were found of the suspect holding handguns and posing in front of a car that matched the description given by witnesses at the scene of the shooting. In a matter of days, a suspect was arrested and charged with first-degree assault and armed criminal action.

Xander

The one chair where Linda Gill could sleep in her son's room in SLCH's intensive care unit was situated behind the head of his bed and blocked by the many contraptions monitoring vitals and feeding intravenous lines into his 8-year-old body. Three days after his arrival at the hospital, space finally was carved for her to reach the chair to get some rest. Sleep had been minimal. Xander Gill was unconscious, his face extremely swollen. Among the dozen lines and tubes attached to his body was a spinal fluid drain in the top of his head. The drain was the first step taken by neurosurgeon David Limbrick when Xander arrived in the OR via helicopter from Doniphan, Missouri — what Linda called a "spit spot in the road" about 200 miles south of St. Louis.

He was there because of a pellet gun. Xander had been in the backyard at his home one summer day, shooting cans off of a fence with his brother, Garrett, just as they had done most days since Christmas. Xander had received a pump-action BB gun as a gift along with a cowboy hat and boots. Garrett had been given a pellet gun.

They seemed like harmless toys until the pellet gun discharged with Xander in its path. A hunk of lead caught him on the back of his head, low and to the left side near his hairline. What followed was a race against the clock. Linda took Xander to the local hospital, where an hour later he was loaded into a helicopter for a flight to SLCH. She called her ex-husband, Bobby Crews, in Springfield, Missouri. While both pushed the limits of their speedometers,

135

Xander was having a drain installed and enduring a sequence of life-threatening events they would learn about hours later.

Limbrick was quite clear: Xander was on the brink of death. All Linda and Bobby could do was wait as a boy whose motor typically ran nonstop laid perfectly still longer than anyone had ever seen. But he did put up a fight when two nurses arrived to check his status. As one pumped a device to clear fluid from Xander's lungs, his little body protested ever so slightly.

"He does have my temper," Bobby said, managing a smile.

Before making the drive from Springfield, Bobby made sure he was wearing the black T-shirt Xander had picked for Father's Day. It was emblazoned with the phrase "Dad to the Bone," and a large crucifix, also selected by Xander, dangled in front. Bobby acknowledged that he has a BB in one leg, a remnant of the games he played with childhood friends. Linda's memento of BB gun battles is embedded in perpetuity in her rear end.

Both were raised around guns in rural Missouri, where hunting and the gun culture are part of life for many. BB and pellet guns are considered toys and purchased by adults to be given to young kids. But having discovered the potential for bodily harm, Bobby contacted a St. Louis television station in the days after Xander was injured and arranged to tell the family's precautionary tale in hope of helping someone else avoid a similar circumstance.

Relatives watched the report and were spurred to action. Garrett destroyed his gun by thrashing it against the top of a fence in the yard. He tossed Xander's in the trash. Linda's father, who lives with her and the children, took his three shotguns to a relative's house to be placed under lock and key. Her boyfriend asked his boss to keep his hunting rifle for safekeeping.

"I told my boyfriend, even if it's a plastic gun and the thing shoots water to get it out of my house," she said.

Xander's injury was extreme for an air gun but not out of the ordinary considering the power these weapons pack. BB and pellet guns caused 191,736 injuries in the U.S. from 2001 to 2016 among those 19 and younger with 25,364 linked to violence, according to the Centers for Disease Control and Prevention. These guns were involved in 527 instances of self-harm. Deaths are uncommon, but close calls and the need for hospitalization are not as 6,015 injuries required admittance during that span. That's an average of more than one hospital admission per day for an air gun or BB gun injury over a 16-year period.

With her son added to the statistics, Linda settled in for the prospect of an extensive stay. Her daughter had stuffed some clothes and toiletries into a bag while she was at the hospital in Doniphan. They would have to get her through the duration of Xander's treatment at SLCH. Garrett, meanwhile, was an emotional mess back home. He called each day, along with other relatives, hoping that Xander could hear his voice. On the third day, Linda put the phone to his ear.

"I hope you can hear me," Garrett said. "I miss you. I threw our guns away. We don't need them. We can play with something else, play a different game. But I miss you and love you, and I'm sorry."

* * *

Linda was changing the sheets on the last of seven beds on a Tuesday morning when Xander ran inside, clutching the back of his head. He had been shooting with Garrett in a location approved by the landlord. The house backs up to a 180-acre field, so there was little worry about hitting a living thing as long as the boys were careful of the cows.

Linda was accustomed to the kids getting hurt — "They're country boys. They're rough" — but she was not prepared when Xander said he had been shot. He moved his hand from his bloodied neck, and she quickly applied a washcloth to the wound. All the while he kept talking, explaining that his brother's gun had fired accidentally. Suspecting that an ambulance would take too long, Linda chose to drive to the local hospital. She felt a small degree of comfort because Xander was able to talk, even as Linda cussed at a woman whose driving impeded her. But as she pulled in front of the hospital, she glanced at Xander, who was now in a fetal position on the front seat and unresponsive. She started to shake and scream.

Linda was helpless as her son lay unconscious. She had undergone surgery three weeks earlier, leaving her incapable of lifting him from the car. At the hospital, she cried for someone to help Xander, who had waited on her after surgery and routinely helped check her blood sugar daily by pricking her finger. An hour after he was carried into the hospital, a helicopter from St. Louis arrived. Linda began the drive, ignoring the speed limit, but soon felt sick and pulled onto the shoulder of the road. By the time she arrived from the south and Bobby from the southwest, Xander was in surgery.

The initial consultation was blunt: There was a chance Xander wouldn't survive. Bobby was silent before bursting into tears as his legs buckled in a hospital hall.

* * *

Limbrick was tending to patients when he received word that a young boy, who had been shot point blank in the back of the head, was en route. He knew little else other than being told the weapon was an air gun and that the patient had a rating of three on the Glasgow Coma Scale, the lowest possible score. Xander's arrival sent Limbrick scurrying to analyze the results of a CT scan that had arrived electronically. He needed to know if Xander was stable enough to endure surgery. His chance for survival was immediately deemed to be low.

There were questions to answer and quickly. Limbrick had to analyze Xander's chance for survival. Could he breathe if the rate of the ventilator was slowed? Did he have corneal response? Did he have movement in his arms if stimulated by a light pinch? Any of these are signs that the brain is alive and functioning. Limbrick noted that one of Xander's corneas reacted, and he could breathe over the ventilator.

The scan revealed the extent of the problem that Limbrick and a massive crew would face in the OR. The pellet had entered Xander's neck close to a vertebral artery as it passed through the C1 vertebra, which supports the globe of the head. A couple of millimeters in the wrong direction and he could have suffered a stroke and died. When the pellet entered, it struck at the base of his skull and shattered into fragments. The largest portion of the pellet deflected downward toward the C1. The force triggered bleeding, which caused swelling in his cerebellum, which in turn compressed his brain stem and spinal fluid channel. The result was obstructive hydrocephalus, a condition that creates an unacceptable accumulation of spinal fluid in the ventricles. Thus, the drain was necessary.

After a portion of Xander's head was shaved, Limbrick immediately made a small incision along the coronal suture — a dense connective tissue. He then used a small hand drill to create a hole in the skull, open a membrane inside the skull but outside the brain, and insert a catheter. The drain was inserted and secured within 15 minutes.

Because the accident occurred during the day, there was an abundance of help available. The room was more chaotic than most OR scenes with 18 people rushing about to expedite every move. Xander was now ready to be positioned for the surgery, and this is when the extra personnel paid dividends. However, seconds after being turned onto his stomach, Xander went into cardiac arrest. He quickly was returned to his back, and six anesthesiologists converged, working frantically. Five minutes later a disaster had been averted. Xander had been stabilized but was in a far more precarious state.

"The anesthesiologists saved his life, without any question," Limbrick said later in his office. "I thought he wasn't going to survive. Then you have to make a decision. He's stable enough, so should we try to turn him over and operate? They said, 'What do you want to do?' Am I putting him at more risk by operating on him? It's not black or white. But in this case he would have died without it. So I felt like the best thing was to give him a chance."

Limbrick didn't have time to debate the pros and cons with the staff or ponder the decision over coffee. Xander had a blood clot that needed to be removed, had nearly died on the table and had fluid in his breathing tube, causing further concerns. Limbrick decided quickly to proceed and realized the surgery needed to be expedited.

With Xander now on his stomach a second time, Limbrick made an incision in his upper neck, slicing upward and curving to the left. He used electrocautery to cut through muscle to reach the surface of the skull as blood poured through the incision. Limbrick cut a small chunk of Xander's skull and then removed a clot the size of a golf ball along with some brain tissue. Normally he would have removed more tissue to create additional space for the brain to swell. But he had done what was necessary for his patient to survive.

Forty-one minutes after the start of surgery, Xander was prepared for his trip to the ICU.

"We felt like his chances were still low, but we had done the surgery we were able to do," Limbrick said.

* * *

BB and pellet wounds are not unusual at SLCH. Frequently, the injury involves a BB in or around the eye. Limbrick doesn't get involved unless the damage is intracranial. He usually is intent on removing the object because as a "low-velocity missile" it is not likely to be sterile. However, a year earlier he performed a surgery in which the BB was lodged in a critical area of the brain. He opted to leave it for fear of causing more problems, and the patient survived.

"When someone calls and says 'I have a kid with an intracranial BB,' I don't think it's so weird. I think, 'What are we going to do about it?'" Limbrick said. "Xander is the perfect example of someone who has an injury where the pellet didn't travel inside the brain, yet all the havoc of a major gunshot has been wreaked. The swelling, the pressure on the brain stem, the obstructive hydrocephalus is all stuff we expect with a high-powered injury."

Statistics on air gun deaths are not available. The CDC doesn't keep those numbers, and the U.S. Consumer Product Safety Commission has taken to quoting a figure of four fatalities per year, strictly out of habit to reflect the lack of updated research. However, the CPSC did issue a safety alert in 2012, warning that BB guns with velocities greater than 350 feet per second increase the risk of death, and recommending that children under 16 not use high-velocity BB or pellet guns. There are no federal laws regulating non-powder guns.

Emergency department physician Bo Kennedy recalled the case of a patient who had been shot in the chest with a BB. The situation was dire enough that the victim had to be airlifted 30 miles to the hospital. An ultrasound performed when he arrived showed the BB was in the femoral artery, near the victim's groin, not anywhere near the point of entry. It had gone through the base of the aorta and barely missed the takeoff for the right main coronary artery, which likely would have resulted in death. It then floated around the aorta and traveled to the groin.

"It's an amazing story," Kennedy said. "People think, 'BBs, eh.'"

SLCH has had patients with BBs that have traveled halfway through their brains. In one incident, a boy angry at a friend went home to get his BB gun. He then knocked on the other boy's door and shot him in the belly from close range when he answered.

Kennedy is one of those in the hospital who is so unnerved by guns, so completely in favor of limiting their access, that he once declined to let his twin teenage sons attend a father-son paintball game arranged by friends.

"I wrote back to everybody and said, 'This makes no sense to me,'" he said. "We're teaching our kids how to shoot each other? They just don't get it. Our culture is so oriented toward guns, and people don't understand the impact of being shot."

Surgeon Kate Bernabe recalled being dismayed when a female physician friend wrote on Facebook about her 10-year-old receiving a BB gun as a birthday gift.

"I thought, 'This person's a pediatrician, and she's excited?'" she said. Bernabe had to perform surgery on one patient who was shot in the belly with a BB gun. Another patient had a BB found in his chest during an exam for something unrelated. And yet another had a BB enter through an eye and travel into the brain. "There's a space in the eye and it can go through the tissue, and the next thing you know the brain is right there. Most people don't realize a tiny pellet can cause damage."

Xander was hit by a pellet from a gun with a velocity of 1,300 feet per second. All it takes is a BB or pellet traveling 400 feet per second to break skin. When a projectile reaches 1,300 feet per second, it qualifies as supersonic speed, which is faster than the speed of sound. By comparison, many police officers carry 9-mm handguns, which are subsonic. One significant difference that worked in Xander's favor is that a light projectile such as a pellet, which might be four grains, loses energy quickly when it makes contact with a target.

Xander would recover, but a family had been changed forever.

* * *

Xander was sitting and watching the Disney Channel in his darkened room, the shades pulled tight. Without warning, he leaned forward and began to sob and mutter, "I want my bubby, I want my bubby." He had not seen Garrett since leaving the house for the hospital. The pleas for his brother continued for a minute until he lost strength and collapsed back on the bed.

"Happens every day," Linda told me as she wrapped her arms around Xander's limp body. Four weeks had passed since he arrived on the brink of death. Linda hadn't been home and barely left the hospital except to make short walks to a tiny grocery store for supplies, accompany Xander to a garden or step outside for a smoke. She did laundry on the hospital's first floor, where the service is free except for a 25-cent fee for detergent and fabric softener.

Xander regained consciousness less than a week after surgery, a development that stunned Limbrick. He remained weak, especially on his left side. His room was across the hall from the rehabilitation center. When a nurse arrived, he slowly pulled on his shoes and slid off the bed into a wheelchair that would take him for his next session. There remained no indication of when Xander would go home. Linda knew that being stuck in the hospital was hell for a little boy who does not take kindly to inactivity. He was named after the Vin Diesel character Xander Cage, a thrill-seeking, extreme-sports enthusiast, and had grown appropriately into that energetic role.

He was accustomed to wearing shorts without a shirt or shoes as long as the weather was conducive, and was a budding outdoorsman with a love of yard work. He had his own makeshift push lawn mower, created by his grandfather, who shortened the handle on an old mower so that Xander could cut the grass. Xander used duct tape to attach a flashlight so that he could finish jobs when daylight became sparse. He had talked of becoming a farmer so that he would not be reliant on others for food, or possibly a mechanic to avoid paying others to fix his cars. And he loved living in the country, which is one reason the blinds were drawn in his room.

"He saw the city for the first time, and he cried," Linda said. "He said, 'I want to go back to the woods.' He thought the trees were fake."

Xander would soon be going back to the woods, which wasn't a foregone conclusion when he left surgery. But he figured to regain most of his physical function over time and had already made significant progress.

"There are times you do things like this and people are out of it for weeks or months," Limbrick said. "He made a dramatic recovery. The day after surgery I heard his mom say she thought he was responsive, and I thought she was being optimistic. Then I'd hear about him moving an arm or a leg and thought, 'No way. That's got to be some sort of spinal reflex.' It took a long time to convince me what he was doing was not reflexive. But they were right, and I was wrong. It's hard to describe how fortunate he's been."

Six weeks after the shooting, Garrett was not doing so well. Linda had received reports of people telling him he had killed his brother. After one physical encounter, he was sent to a facility for children with behavioral issues. He required medication. The incident changed the brothers' lives forever, but Linda believed that one day it would be for the better.

The immediate goal was to get Xander home. She told doctors he would be better off doing therapy in Doniphan, surrounded by family and his dog. Days turned into weeks until finally after 45 days, he was cleared to leave the hospital.

First on his to-do list was a fishing trip with his grandpa and uncle Johnny.

Security

The entrance to the emergency room is manned at all times by two armed public safety officers. They are the first people who greet a family, whether the visit is for a hacking cough or a life-threatening injury. For some, it can be disconcerting.

Some officers wear optional bullet-proof vests. They're stationed behind a wall of glass that is decorated with zoo animals that help to partially obscure the view inside the building. Patients enter by passing through a metal detector. This is the world that many hospitals, including children's facilities, face. Sometimes even that degree of protection isn't considered enough by the people working on the front lines and behind the scenes.

By their very nature, medical emergencies are emotional and stressful events. The reactions of families and friends of patients are unpredictable, and hospital violence has escalated over the years. With gunshot cases, the variables can be far more numerous and combustible than with other trauma cases. In some instances, two factions are engaged in violence with the possibility of retaliation. The crowds of relatives and friends who rush to the hospital have been known to swell to uncontrollable numbers. Situations are typically diffused before they can escalate, and that's mainly attributable to the presence of security.

The night 6-year-old Marcus Johnson Jr. arrived in the arms of a bloodied St. Louis police officer presented a test for the hospital. Marcus had been leaving a park in north St. Louis with his family one week after enduring another in a long line of heart surgeries. The family's car was targeted by a group of men, one of whom had a brief argument with Marcus Johnson Sr. in the park. The ensuing flurry of gunfire hit three people in the Johnson's car, including the little boy, his teenage brother and a 69-year-old man. With no time to spare, a responding officer scooped Marcus into his arms and transported him to SLCH.

The police car carrying the child pulled in front of the hospital entrance about 8 p.m., a peak hour for activity in the ER, which was packed with patients. The officer burst through the entrance with Marcus pressed against his blood-soaked shirt. Lacking information about specifics of the shooting, public safety manager Joe Vitale immediately ordered a lockdown in the ER. With the push of a button in the security cubicle, no one could enter or exit through the main entrance. The auxiliary entrances also were locked. Officers from other areas of the hospital arrived as backup to monitor the situation.

"The ER was already full," Vitale said. "We did everything we could. We didn't even know the kid's name. They were giving us as much information as they could. We didn't tell the patients or visitors in the waiting room. They saw the police run through with the kid. We had to assume to worst."

Vitale called for help from officers at neighboring Barnes-Jewish Hospital, which sent officers on bike patrol to watch the exterior at SLCH. Officers from the St. Louis Metropolitan Police Department also arrived. Vitale and his staff had discussed a plan that would be employed when Marcus' parents arrived. It took ER personnel little time to realize that they could not save the boy.

When Marcus Sr. and his wife, Quiana, left police headquarters about 3:30 a.m., they went directly to the hospital. By that point, little Marcus was being taken to the morgue. They arrived to find the doors to the ER locked and were escorted to a small room to wait for a social worker.

"I wanted to see my baby," Marcus Johnson said. "If my baby was dead, let me see him dead. And they never let us see him. When the social worker came I said, 'Thank you. Now I'm getting somewhere.' I could see him and go home in peace. I asked to see him, and they said they couldn't do that."

Marcus was angry and upset. As he exited the building, the emotions triggered an outburst. As another person went through the exit, Marcus ran back into the ER through the open door. A verbal confrontation ensued, and more officers were called to the area. "The family escalated the situation because they wanted to see their kid," Vitale said. "It's very sensitive. You don't want everyone in the EU and waiting room upset because these people are losing their minds because they're in grief. It's a fine line."

When Marcus Johnson calmed down, he apologized and went home. One son was dead, another in the hospital with a gunshot wound. His car was riddled with bullet holes, and the shooters were still at large.

* * *

Security at hospitals is serious and big business. The enterprise is now so large that an organization exists called the International Association for Healthcare Security & Safety.

Surgeons have been accosted and even killed by former patients and relatives of patients. Not long after a heart surgeon was shot and killed at Brigham and Women's Hospital in Boston in 2015, SLCH implemented a new system that requires personnel to use security cards to enter stairwells that were previously accessible by most anyone.

When a gunshot patient arrives, a number of possible scenarios must be considered by security personnel, of which there are eight on duty at any given time throughout the hospital. The victim sometimes is accompanied in the ambulance by relatives. This prompts an officer to enter the ambulance bay to check them with a metal-detecting wand before they can enter the trauma bay. The patient must be checked for weapons, and those searches have turned up knives, brass knuckles and mace, among other things. Nurses and doctors search for tattoos that could indicate a gang affiliation. The number of friends and relatives to gather outside the ER has been known to grow as large as 30 or 40, sometimes requiring crowd-control measures.

Patients frequently are placed on involuntary protective status, also referred to as blackout status. They are registered under a pseudonym. Their presence cannot be confirmed to anyone calling the hospital, and they are limited to four visitors. Each approved visitor is photographed, and copies of the photos are given to the nursing staff to check upon' arrival. Cell phones are prohibited in the hospital rooms of IPS patients. Break the rules and you can be removed from protected status.

Protective status also can be voluntary. Such was the case in late 2014 when a child pulled a gun out of the couch at his house and accidentally shot himself. Because one of the boy's relatives had a high profile in the community, the family asked for a blackout to avoid media coverage.

It can be difficult to keep family and friends off of social media, where information about patients often spreads. People close to the victim want information, and they sometimes flood the hospital with crowds that must be monitored. One night when a teenage boy was shot, a group in the first-floor lobby ebbed and flowed with at least 15 people lingering for more than an hour. An emotional young boy repeatedly blamed himself for the incident. It was a mostly calm gathering near an entrance manned by one security officer. A door to the ER treatment rooms was just around the corner. When members of the crowd started a verbal confrontation with the officer, everyone was asked to leave.

On some occasions, officers are assigned to sit outside a patient's room, which can occur if a patient is an elopement risk or being watched for suicidal tendencies. Entire floors have been known to go on lockdown. That happened a few weeks before Marcus was killed. The individuals coming and going on the floor where a gunshot patient was staying were controlled to the point that other patients needed approval to move about.

"It lasted two days until the police came back," Vitale said. "But there was a legitimate threat. A guy had shot the patient once, and he was still on the loose. Whenever a detective tells us there's a legitimate threat, we take that very seriously."

Surgeon Kate Bernabe was always hyper-aware of the presence of police officers and security risks she felt in some situations involving GSW patients. Arriving in the morning for rounds and finding the doors to a specific floor locked was not out of the ordinary. She knew there was only one reason. She treated shooting victims who were handcuffed to their beds — even in intensive care — with officers stationed outside the rooms. She didn't necessarily fear the patient but rather a potential emergency situation that might require the patient to be moved at a moment's notice. She has performed surgery with four officers waiting outside the OR, sitting at desks in their uniforms.

But Bernabe was most paranoid about the trauma bay when a patient first arrived. She would find herself thinking about scenarios and how they should be handled, especially when she was pregnant. The presence of ER security allowed for a degree of comfort, but she liked to be mentally prepared.

"I would think and prepare myself, just making sure the situation was safe," she said. "I don't think everyone thinks about that every time to make sure a situation is secure. I would think about whether the doors were closed. Who's in the room? I always wanted the least amount of people in the room. We've dealt with violent and hostile family members, and I didn't want to be in a situation where I had to worry about that. I wanted to make sure that when a GSW came in, there were people acutely aware to make sure the situation was safe."

It is on the ground level of the ER where tensions can run the highest. Although nothing as dangerous as a shooting near the ER has ever occurred, some personnel admit they have wondered if the waiting area is a bit too exposed or easily accessed. The occasional scenario where a shooting victim is dropped off by friends or dumped outside the ER can heighten nerves and paranoia.

Former public safety manager Terry Kowalczyk handled such an incident when a car pulled up with a teenager who had been shot from behind while sitting in the backseat. Three friends dragged him into the ER and were then held for St. Louis police to question. The car was seized because it had signs of bullet holes in the exterior.

"I still actually worry about a gunshot patient coming into the trauma bay and someone following that person in there to make sure that person is done," Bernabe said a year before she left the hospital.

Kowalczyk considered the fear of gunshots coming from outside the hospital to be irrational. The street that leads to the hospital's parking garage and main entrance is a short dead end. He argued that no one would risk being trapped just to fire a couple of shots.

Johns Hopkins Hospital personnel in Baltimore studied hospital shootings after an incident in 2010. The results showed that while such shootings are uncommon, there were 154 incidents nationally that resulted in 235 deaths or injuries during an 11-year period. The study concluded that 30 percent of the hospital shootings occurred in the emergency room and that half of those involved a security officer's gun that had been stolen or used by the officer. The research showed that officer training could be more helpful than money spent on technology to search for weapons.

"I've never seen a retaliation while doing hospital security, but then we didn't know Ferguson was going to blow up either," said Vitale in 2015 after replacing Kowalczyk. "We do hazardous vulnerability assessments and look at everything at the facility related to threats. We rate civil unrest. Well, for four years we didn't have any civil unrest. It was always zero or one on a scale of one to five. Now, it's probably a six."

Social worker Margie Batek has experienced the risks that exist behind the scenes on more than once occasion. She and her staff routinely talk to family members in rooms tucked deep inside the ER. The questions are often personal and probing, and they are asked as soon after a shooting incident as possible. Batek sometimes has wondered if the person on the other side of the table had a weapon. Few people were more thrilled when the metal detector was installed at the entrance.

"There have been times through the years when I've looked back and thought 'I'm lucky I'm still alive' with some of the people we've encountered," she said. "They come in stressed, and it may have involved something illegal. They're afraid they'll be turned over to law enforcement."

She has seen parents punch holes in walls and throw furniture. She learned to position herself safely in the small rooms where interviews take place and to watch body language closely, especially in the days before the metal detector. Batek worked for five years as an investigator and said she never was touched. The first time she was struck was at SLCH when a distraught mother punched her in the head. A male nurse happened to be passing the room and backed the woman into a corner until she could be calmed.

Another night, Batek was working when an infant was shot and driven to the hospital by a man and woman. She took them to a small room that was a good distance from the treatment area. There was enough space in the room for a chair and small sofa, where the couple sat. The man repeatedly told the woman they needed time to talk in private. Batek sensed tension and the possibility of a problem. The mother's clothes had been splattered with the baby's blood. Meanwhile, Batek sought information on the shooting, which supposedly had occurred in a drive-by.

"All of a sudden she jumps up and says, 'You shot my baby,'" Batek said. "I realized it might have been in a car, but he was probably shooting at someone, and the kid got hit. I didn't know if he was still carrying the gun. He freaks out, jumps up and starts running into the hall, and I'm yelling for security."

Out of 38 officers employed by the hospital in 2015, 50 percent were former police officers, 30 percent had served in a branch of the military, and the remainder had experience as security officers. All but four carried .38-caliber pistols. The others were cleared not to carry weapons. Future hires were to be required to do so, however. A risk-assessment study had cleared the unarmed officers. Vitale figured it was not an issue because, by his calculations, 90 percent of the job is customer-service related. Officers check badges, give directions, offer friendly smiles. It's the 10 percent that involves de-escalation of potentially dangerous situations that are of concern.

After 23 years, Kenneth Robinson was at the tail end of his career. He started at Barnes-Jewish but moved to SLCH for the final years before retirement, figuring he'd see fewer physical confrontations as he got older. That was the case. Barnes-Jewish has about 3,200 trauma admissions every year of which an average of 16 percent are penetrating wounds. That makes for 500 or so GSWs every year, or an average of more than one per day. Whether it was gunshot trauma or other high-tension scenarios, the chances of an altercation were always significant for Robinson. Toward the end of his tenure at Barnes, he had to break up a fight and broke a bone in his hand.

"There was a lot going on over there, that's for sure," he said. "That's the reason I came over here. I'm getting older. When I was younger with the stuff that went on at the Barnes emergency room, I could handle it and didn't get hurt as much. I transferred because of that last incident. I said it's time to do something else so I can last the rest of these years."

Robinson still knows the potential for escalation and appreciates the precautions. The security staff has been trained for the possibility of an armed intruder. The hospital was on heightened alert during the Ferguson protests and the night that a decision from the grand jury was delivered in the Michael Brown case. More officers were scheduled, and shifts were extended. The possibility of injuries from civil unrest had to be considered along with the chance of potential unrest spilling into the area near the hospital.

On that same night, Vitale and another officer drove to the Ronald McDonald House near Cardinal Glennon Hospital to pick up the family of a child who was going to have a transplant at SLCH. At the same time, protesters were attempting to shut down Interstate 44 by blocking the highway, which is one of the possible routes between the two hospitals.

But at SLCH all remained calm.

* * *

When he was 4 months old, Marcus Johnson Jr. was diagnosed with Kawasaki Disease, which causes inflammation in the walls of arteries. He had undergone one of numerous surgeries and been released from the hospital a week before the shooting. Marcus lived with the disease for six years as if it were a minor nuisance. He knew his dietary restrictions — no lemons or oranges and a tight rein on fried foods — and stuck to the rules. He knew his physical limitations.

On a beautiful day in March 2015, the family visited O'Fallon Park, where two men were found shot to death in a car several months earlier. The park was outside of the neighborhood where the Johnsons lived. The family's presence didn't sit well with one of the shooters, who suggested to Marcus Sr. that he needed to leave.

"He said I was holding up traffic in his hood," Marcus said. "I said, 'We're in a park.' He's like, 'You think I'm playing with you?' After that, I called the kids and told them we were going."

As they prepared to leave, Quiana saw the man, with a gun in his hand, headed to a car with a group of people. The Johnson's Pontiac minivan turned out of the park onto West Florissant Avenue and stopped at a red light. When the light changed, Quiana turned and saw a car exiting the park and heading in the same direction. Marcus checked his rearview mirror and saw multiple cars approaching at a high rate of speed. Quiana told him to go through the light at Taylor Avenue, but the other cars had closed the gap and the shooting started. Quiana's oldest son was struck in the right ankle. An elderly friend was struck in the knee. Marcus was hit in the torso.

Marcus and Quiana had a newly purchased handgun in the car. Quiana handed the gun to her husband as he drove on tires flattened by bullets. He pointed the gun aimlessly out the driver's side window, firing several shots high and to the rear of the van. He continued to drive until reaching a relative's house about 10 blocks from the park. Everyone piled into the house, and the police were called. Officers arrived before the ambulance. One grabbed Marcus Jr., placed him in his car and headed to SLCH.

"I already knew," Quiana said. "Even when they were still shooting, I said, 'Forget it.' Bullets were flying past me. His eyes rolled back in his head, and all I could do was pick my baby up and hold him. He was gone, right then and there."

As the police cruiser carrying Marcus made its way through the streets of north St. Louis, other officers blocked intersections to provide a clear path. The car pulled up outside the ER entrance. The officer grabbed Marcus and held him tight to his body before rushing through the crowded waiting area. Officer Don Re arrived in another car. Later that night, Re wrote in his personal blog about the incident. The blog went viral.

"We hurried into the emergency room, where we were met by the trauma team and hospital staff," he wrote. "I'm always in awe at how these emergency room doctors and nurses and staff are so able to get to working on a patient so fast.

"There was some sliver of hope that the boy would make it, at least that's what we all wanted to believe.

"The truth, and I think we all knew it, was that this boy would never fall asleep in his own bed again. When the officer laid the boy down on the gurney and stood back upright, any wind that may have been in my sails quickly faded to nothing.

"His shirt said it all."

Re's blog was a heartfelt plea for something to change. The rash of shootings in St. Louis was bad enough, but its impact on children was overwhelming Re and his co-workers, who responded to calls like this with far too much regularity.

Not long after arriving, Re and the other officers left SLCH, knowing the outcome was as they had suspected.

"To go back to my car, I had to walk past the same group of people who were in the waiting room when we walked past them earlier with the dying boy," he wrote in his blog. "Three little boys grabbed at me and asked me if that boy we carried in earlier was dead.

"'Did he die, officer? Was that boy dead?' They asked me.

"I got no help from their mom, as she was tending to a clearly sick kid of her own. "'Boys, he's fine. He's a strong boy, just like you guys.'

"I felt bad lying, but it seemed easier than having to explain death to three strange kids all under 10 years old.

"I went to my car and grabbed a bunch of Dum-Dums from the bag I carry around. Mom was cool with me giving them suckers, and they left me alone about the dead boy they still thought was alive.

"I couldn't tell them that the boy who was about their same age had straight-lined. "Five-year-olds shouldn't straight line.

"Why did this one?

"Because of gun violence in the city.

"The weather was nice so the people were out. "Some people were out with their guns.

"Why did this boy have to die? "Was it disrespect?

"Drugs?

"A woman? "Money?

"All stupid reasons to fire a gun anywhere near another human being, let alone children, but here we are again, with another child lost to violence."

While the officers were at the hospital, and even as Re was at home writing his blog at 2 a.m., Marcus and Quiana were being interviewed by police. But all they wanted was to find out about their children. When the interview finally ended, they drove to SLCH.

"We got to the emergency room, and they wouldn't let us in the door," Marcus said. "I was mad already because I sat in that interrogation room after I knew two of my kids were injured. I had a lot on my mind. They called every security guard on me."

First Responders

The logistics of emergency medical services in the St. Louis region are complicated by the vast number of agencies that have saturated the market. Achieving consistency in treatment, response times and choice of facilities is difficult because at least 140 ambulance entities serve a 150-mile radius. Many of St. Louis County's 88 municipalities have their own ambulance services. In some cases, neighboring cities share. Some are private companies that serve the city and county. Some, such as Christian EMS, are operated by local hospitals and have specific areas of service. And the city of St. Louis has a fleet of ambulances available for calls within the city limits.

Confusion abounds about why some older teens end up at SLCH and some next door at Barnes-Jewish. Or how the determination is made between SLCH, Cardinal Glennon and other hospitals where kids and teens can be transported. That's in part because protocols are different from one ambulance service to another.

"They see a lot of 16-year-olds and 17-year-olds across the street," Dr. Pat Dillon said of Barnes-Jewish. "And why EMS decides on one place or the other has long been sort of a mystery."

SLCH encourages EMS to take gunshot patients to its emergency room. It's like any business that markets itself and the services and products it has to offer. The emphasis has been altered dramatically since the days when Dillon was trying to keep his head above water. At one point overwhelmed and hoping to send more patients next door, the hospital sells itself as a leader in trauma and a facility that can best handle all levels of injuries within its demographics. When you have a specialty you sell it, and no children's hospital has more experience in this area. They're not putting it on billboards or flyers, but they get the information to the people who make the decisions about where a child will be transported.

St. Louis enjoys the luxury of having two Level 1 pediatric trauma centers. SLCH and Cardinal Glennon are fewer than three miles apart, but the volume of gunshot trauma cases at each is significantly different. The two hospitals are separated by Interstate 64, a division that can help dictate which hospital gets a patient. Sometimes the decision is as simple as which direction the ambulance is facing when it leaves the scene of a shooting. If a turnaround on a major road can be avoided, it might save enough time that driving to the more distant hospital becomes an advantage.

Unfortunately, the St. Louis metro area has more than enough gunshot cases to go around. In the city alone, where the population sits near 308,000, homicides jumped to 205 in 2017, up from 113 in 2012. Thus, it is not a surprise that St. Louis ends up being listed among the most dangerous cities in the United States on a regular basis (although such rankings and the statistics they are based upon are challenged by civic leaders). The majority of homicides are of adults. Many of the younger victims fall into the murky area of being transported either to a children's or an adult hospital.

The official pediatric age cutoff in Missouri is 15, and Barnes-Jewish is open to taking any trauma patients who have reached that age. Because SLCH officially will accept patients to the age of 21, a considerable overlap occurs. A Venn diagram depicting the gunshot patients who could go to SLCH and those who could go to Barnes-Jewish would include a sizeable intersection. That's where confusion exists.

From the start of 2008 to the end of 2016, Barnes-Jewish treated 534 patients who were 19 or younger. In the same span, SLCH treated 350 in the 15-to-19 age group. Theoretically, any of those 884 patients could have gone to the children's hospital.

"I think EMS realizes when they're 'gangbangers' and brings them over here," said Douglas Schuerer, director of trauma services at Barnes-Jewish. "Children's has 1- and 2-year-olds and doesn't need 17-year-olds. When it's interpersonal kid violence or unintentional, that's a little different. The accidents in the home and suicide attempts — we get all of that because we take 15 and up. But there is a mix, and where they go a lot of times is based on not knowing how old they are."

Schuerer represents the conflicting opinions. Although inundated by GSWs on a regular basis, he is willing to have Barnes-Jewish take more by treating the older teens. Schuerer and his staff see about 500 gunshot cases annually, so adding the overflow wouldn't add significantly to the workload.

There are many reasons why older patients end up at SLCH or younger patients at Barnes-Jewish. In many cases, age is difficult to determine, and young patients can appear to be much older than their age due to size, tattoos or facial hair. Sometimes the circumstances of the shooting are viewed as adult behavior and, thus, worthy of adult care. Some patients lie about their age because they prefer to go to the children's hospital. When patients are driven to the hospital by family or friends, the entrances to the hospitals can be confused.

The American Academy of Pediatrics says that patients up to the age of 18 are minors and should go to pediatric facilities. It is the job of Rich Dandridge, the pre-hospital outreach coordinator, to address some of the issues related to age and how to best handle patients. Some of his work is purely marketing to generate more business. He also promotes the hospital's status as being verified by the American College of Surgeons. Soon after Keller arrived, the hospital achieved ACS verification, attesting that the hospital has optimal resources for trauma care. It doesn't hurt Dandridge's case when he can tell EMTs and paramedics that data show an 11 percent improvement on mortality at ACS-verified Level 1 trauma centers.

"There is a variety of reasons a pediatric patient gets better care at a pediatric facility," Dandridge said. "When I was 18, I was 270 pounds when I played college football as a freshman. But they should be coming to us because while you may be physically that large, emotionally you still need all the backside support of what a pediatric patient needs. Emotional needs aren't going to be met at an adult hospital."

About 500 ambulances delivered patients to SLCH every month as of 2012. That was an increase of 50 to 75 ambulances from the previous decade. It was a jump that arguably could be attributed partly to the rise in the number of kids injured by guns during that time. But whether they end up in the children's or adult hospital, a point of agreement is that gunshot wounds need to be treated at Level 1 trauma centers. There are many hospitals in the St. Louis area where an ambulance can take a wounded patient, depending on where the incident occurred.

"Previously, there were hospitals that would boast that they're level 1 or 2 trauma centers for children, when they haven't met the requirements," said Brad Warner, the hospital's chief of surgery. "Marty knows what it takes to qualify and has focused on getting a little more clarity on those things. Is it good enough to say you're a pediatric trauma center when you don't have anyone with pediatric experience?"

There are guidelines that dictate where severely injured patients should be delivered. The Time Critical Diagnosis statute was passed in Missouri in 2008 after being initiated by Dr. John William Jermyn III, an emergency physician at Barnes-Jewish. The legislation was passed one day after Jermyn died and took years to be implemented. It covers trauma, stroke and heart attack with specific guidelines for each. The regulations for all three cover nearly 300 pages, but Keller can sum up the point of the legislation in a matter of words.

"It's really to get the sickest of the sick to the highest level of care that's needed," he said.

If a gunshot patient is in dire need of attention, the question always has been: Should the ambulance stop at the closest hospital, regardless of its level of care? Or should it take the extra time necessary, within reason, to reach a top-flight facility that is best equipped to handle those types of injuries? In some cases, such difficult decisions must be made in the heat of the moment. Often, a patient's life is at stake.

"Hopefully it's being utilized," Keller said of the time critical diagnosis. "I haven't seen changes in volume. It's really for the sickest of the sick. It has been a problem since I've been in this state. I can't point fingers at what I consider malpractice, but there have been cases where I think a patient clearly had inappropriate care before they were transferred to us, whether or not the patient would have survived."

Once such instance in 2015 involved a young girl who was shot in north St. Louis County. The ambulance took her to Christian Hospital, which was four miles closer than SLCH. She regained vital signs and was then transferred but died that night. The initial choice of hospitals had to be made quickly. Christian, however, is not a trauma center.

"If they took a critical gunshot wound to Christian, they'd have some explaining to do, for sure," said Dr. David Tan, who is chief of the EMS section at Washington University and has extensive experience as a medical director for St. Louis-area fire, ambulance and police agencies. "By and large, even the north county gunshots will go the extra miles to Barnes or Children's rather than to Christian."

Besides delays, other problems can arise if a patient with a GSW goes to a lower-tier facility or an adult hospital. Children taken to nonpediatric hospitals frequently are exposed to unnecessary and extensive X-rays or CT scans that can be inappropriate for young patients. A study by Saint Louis University Hospital published in 2016 looked at inefficiencies in imaging when involved in the transfer of pediatric patients. Among the conclusions was that the initial imaging "leads to excess ionizing radiation, and increased health-care costs." There are also indications that pediatric patients are more likely to receive unnecessary surgery at adult hospitals.

"Any time you stop at another hospital, it delays definitive care," Keller said. "They feel like they need to do stuff. If you know you're going to move them out of the hospital, you don't need to do advanced imaging. Adults get CAT scans head to toe, and we never do that with children."

In terms of treatment of trauma in the field, not a lot has changed in the last couple of decades. The key goals are to stop the bleeding, start an IV, maintain the airway and get to a hospital as quickly as possible. Paramedics want to get trauma patients under a doctor's care as soon as possible.

Twenty minutes is the maximum that should be spent at a scene. An explanation is required on the trip sheet if a stop takes longer. Tan enforces similar protocols within all of the agencies he oversees and said, "My best can be off the scene in less than 10 minutes." The national median prehospital time for pediatric gunshot trauma cases in 2016 was 35 minutes, according to the National Trauma Data Bank, the shortest time for any type of injury.

Tan is a Washington University faculty member who oversees a half-dozen EMS physicians at Barnes-Jewish and is responsible for the oversight of two dozen EMS/air medical/emergency dispatch agencies. He has high standards for quick work at the scene of a shooting. When he's training people, it is a point of emphasis. Thus, he is frustrated that similar goals can't be implemented throughout the St. Louis area. The task would involve nearly 80 jurisdictions in the city and county alone, each with its own protocols, medical directors and policies.

"It's a nightmare," Tan said. "Some have very little to no quality-assurance program and might not comply with the latest guidelines. As one who holds employees accountable, that's a major difference."

One of the most significant changes in EMS over the years has been a move to have medics declare more deaths in the field without taking patients to a hospital. Otherwise, the numbers seen at SLCH would be slightly higher. In the past, paramedics were instructed to get all patients to a hospital, the preference being that someone else make the call regarding deaths.

"The training is better now, and they realized the amount of money being spent on health care," Vance said. "The minute you put them in the ambulance, it's $250. Go through the doors of the ER, and it's another $100. Then you start pumping all this medicine into them, and for what? The end result is the same. There's also an ethical consideration. Is it ethical to take someone who's obviously dead, start pumping on their chest and sticking all these tubes and needles into them when the result is going to be the same?"

* * *

SLCH has taken significant steps to help train paramedics and EMTs when it comes to handling trauma cases, especially those involving gun wounds. Dandridge, in conjunction with Cardinal Glennon, received a grant in 2014 that allowed the two hospitals to offer trauma education for 96 providers that serve St. Louis-area hospitals. His predecessor was involved in 104 such classes several years earlier. Training specific to trauma is a limited commodity for EMS providers. It is even more minimal when it comes to preparation to treat pediatric trauma patients.

The American Academy of Pediatrics addressed pre-hospital care in its policy statement on the management of pediatric trauma. In doing so, the statement noted, "Pre-hospital providers may not be as familiar with effective pediatric emergency care as they are with the care provided to adults because most pre-hospital providers are infrequently exposed to critically ill or injured children."

Keller was involved in extensive trauma education in rural areas of Missouri and Illinois during his initial years at the hospital. Trauma manager Diana Kraus would drive him to far-flung locales such as Sikeston, Perryville, Columbia, Washington, Rolla and Hannibal in Missouri to talk about trauma care. He went to Quincy, Carbondale and Effingham in Illinois. The trips were routine and Keller was known to complain. He once asked Vance, "Why does Warner get to go to Europe, and you're dragging me to Perryville?"

Vance always suspected Keller's protests were mostly an act. "He'll complain a lot, but he really seemed to enjoy it and he did a really good job," Vance said. "And the thing is, a lot of his talks he kind of did on the fly. We'd be driving and he'd be putting his talk together."

Keller says he dislikes speaking to large groups, but he's actually quite effective, if not dynamic. Whether addressing small groups of EMS providers, medical students at Washington University or residents and nurses at the hospital, Keller speaks with the confidence of someone with vast knowledge and experience, to the point that he is not the least bit uncomfortable injecting opinions that can be controversial.

I saw several of his presentations, including at an EMS conference in north St. Louis, the heart of considerable gun violence. Keller's talk came complete with a slide show that alternately displayed statistics, points on patient care and photos, including one of Trevin Gamble and his mother during the teen's early stages of recovery. He listed some of what he considered the most absurd ways that kids had been shot and gave a brief synopsis of the attempt to save the life of a 10-year-old shot by his mother. He repeatedly emphasized his belief that every shooting is preventable.

Keller used his EMS presentations as a rallying cry as well as a teaching opportunity. He doesn't dwell on societal issues or his dislike for guns, but when he's done there isn't much question about where he stands. At one talk, he did reference strides that he felt were made in Missouri after handgun buyers were required to undergo background checks. That law has since been repealed.

"I hope this is good for what you do and maybe gets you angry, not at me but at everybody, and you help join the cause and see why it's such an important thing we're tackling," Keller told his class. "The most important part of the talk is what we can do to prevent this. There are two approaches: You can bury your head in the sand, or you can take action and, hopefully, this gets you angry."

Reactions from those in attendance at his seminars vary depending on the location. In St. Louis, there is rarely a negative response because the people he addresses have seen the problem first hand. But when he speaks in more rural areas, the reactions can be quite different.

He told me about receiving an NRA application in the mail from someone who had attended one of his classes in Springfield, Missouri. He promptly dropped it in the trash. After presenting in Carbondale, Illinois, comment sheets were returned with several responses that made it clear a few attendees did not appreciate segments of Keller's discussion.

"Obviously against guns," one commenter wrote.

"Too much emphasis on guns in America. Feel like presenter was pushing his beliefs about too many guns in U.S., not on topic of children's injuries and treatment. Did not appreciate it!" said another.

"Dr. Keller's sermon was not on peds trauma. Never interested in hearing him again."

Sara

Dawn didn't know her 11-year-old son had pulled the shotgun from the rack on the wall until she heard him cock the 20-gauge. Before she could process what was happening, her hands were covered in blood, and her 6-year-old daughter's midsection was obliterated. Sara had been sitting on the bed, playing with her mother after a bath. Now she sat bloodied and silent.

"She didn't do anything," Dawn, said. "She didn't start crying. She wasn't screaming. There was no reaction from her. It was weird that there was nothing from her. She just looked at me."

If Dawn could do anything, it would be to erase the images burned into her memory. Her son holding the shotgun. Her daughter's pelvis blown away. The blood.

The night of January 1, 2014, had been quietly winding to a close. Sara and her brother were to return to school the next morning after the holiday break. As always, two shotguns rested on a rack on the wall over a dresser. The kids had been told never to touch them. Otherwise, they weren't a concern, serving more as a wall ornament like a painting or a mirror. Dawn didn't think they were loaded. She had her back to her son as he climbed high enough to pull one from the wall.

The photos on Dr. Albert Woo's computer portray the images that Dawn wants to erase. The blast blew a hole in Sara's pubic region, went through her vagina and tore through her buttocks. The damage was so extensive that a urologist initially was unable to find her urethra. After Sara survived the initial trauma, Woo's job, along with other surgeons, was to put her back together.

As a plastic surgeon at Washington University School of Medicine, Woo dealt with dozens of cases each year during his tenure at SLCH and Barnes-Jewish that required his specialization. The cases weren't typically this gruesome or extensive. He mostly saw hand injuries from guns. Occasionally he saw facial wounds.

"A plastic surgeon is disaster control," he said. "We have this giant wound in this poor girl's groin. X-rays show there is buckshot everywhere. Hundreds of little pellets scattered through her pelvis and right leg. We deal with it the best we can to figure out what's damaged and what's not."

* * *

Sara's brother, the boy who pulled the trigger, ran to the landlord's house across the street for help. Dawn grabbed a blanket and applied it to Sara's massive wound in the hope that pressure would slow the blood loss. Their home is near a fire station but a good 20 minutes from a hospital in Springfield, which is 200 miles from St. Louis in the southwest corner of the state.

As Sara was leaving in an ambulance, Dawn raced for her truck but was intercepted by police. She was told she could not leave the scene. There were questions to answer, so she returned to the house in her blood-splattered clothes. It wasn't until an hour later that she was cleared to go to the hospital, where her mother and sister were waiting with Dawn's younger son.

After the accident, Dawn felt her family being splintered. The 11-year-old was taken to Lakeland Behavioral Health System, which provides psychiatric services. Her younger son went to Boys and Girls Town, where youth with emotional disturbances, post-traumatic stress disorder and other issues receive needed support. Dawn's husband decided he wanted a divorce, and she eventually quit her job at Dollar General. The Department of Family Services visited her home. She faced months of challenges to keep her children with her.

"I thought my life had completely and utterly fallen apart," she said.

But Sara was the focus. The morning after the incident, she was transported by helicopter to SLCH. She had four surgeries in her first 13 days in St. Louis. Dr. Woo was joined by a general surgeon and a urologist for the first operation on January 3, when he tacked the remaining skin back together. There was more plastic surgery on January 6, when Woo began looking for skin elsewhere on Sara's body to help cover the wounds. She also received a colostomy, but surgeons were unable to completely close her belly and it was left partially open. It wasn't closed until September. Her anus was reconstructed on January 9. The initial flurry of procedures ended January 14.

While other surgeons made sure Sara would be able to function as normally as possible, Woo continually worked on reconstruction, including the formation of a new vagina. He initially re-attached what skin remained with the understanding that much of that skin would not survive. Given a week or two, that skin would either live or die and Woo could proceed.

Woo has dealt with an array of injuries. There was a woman whose entire lower face was blown off by her son-in-law. Toward the end of Sara's case, he was involved with a 4-year-old who found a gun in the home and fired a shot that ripped a hole in his skull. He treated one older man repeatedly during a lifetime that saw him shot more than 20 times.

"Gunshot wounds destroy everything in the way," Woo said. "Shotgun wounds are the worst. Everything gets destroyed in its wake."

Woo asked the other surgeons not to damage the skin on the right side of Sara's belly so that it would be available to reconstruct her groin. He eventually used what is known as the vertical rectus abdominis to do just that. By cutting this flap of muscle and skin and pulling it through from the inside, Woo was able to cover a large portion of the wounded area and give Sara a more normal appearance. He took a skin graft from her leg for further reconstruction.

"Aside from the scarring, it's just really amazing," Dawn said.

Sara had arrived at SLCH riddled with buckshot. However, attempts to remove all of the pellets can lead to more problems, so she left with 50 to 75 remaining in her body. Fortunately, the buckshot did not create an infection. Sara returned to school in late February after a fifth surgery and less than two months after the incident.

"Kids are remarkably resilient," Woo said. "They don't know enough to be severely concerned about their future. It's really the parents who are distraught. It really was a matter of dealing with her pain, keeping her comfortable and she did great. By and large, she did surprisingly well for someone who lost most of her perineum. At least she'll have a pretty darn normal life."

Breaking The Cycle

A common phrase Keller uses is "once a victim, always a victim." Although seemingly extreme, the truth is that many victims of gunshots end up returning to the hospital with another GSW or injuries resulting from other forms of violence. The recidivism for penetrating trauma at SLCH was near 10 percent when Keller arrived. Studies around the country have shown similar or higher rates at other hospitals. The chance of death also increases after someone is shot once. When a patient returns to the environment where a shooting took place, there is every reason to believe it could happen again.

Once a victim, always a victim.

Margie Batek saw this trend develop over a long period — longer than Keller. Having grown tired of the pattern, the long-time social worker was determined to find a way to help children who experienced interpersonal violence steer clear of the trappings that led to their injuries and repeat injuries. She had ideas but limited resources.

She came to realize that the best way to gain the confidence of a victim or a family was to be present in the emergency room when they arrived. Reaching them at a vulnerable moment frequently made them more willing to accept help and be open to change. Wait for weeks or months to make contact, and those traumatic memories fade, leaving families far less likely to welcome any type of help.

"They are vulnerable when they come in because they're hurt," she said. "For some, it's the second or third time. It's not unusual to have a kid who's been shot, who's 17 years old, and when I say I need to go see another patient, they say 'Don't leave me.' They're very much children at that point and very vulnerable.

"They see us as nonthreatening. We're not dressed in scrubs or doing anything painful to them. We usually approach from a nurturing perspective, which is something many of them are not used to from people in the system. We're their advocate and let them know that."

Those experiences led to Batek's Victims of Violence Program. It started as a short-term study that was greeted with mild enthusiasm from patients passing through the hospital. But persistence and increased funding led to a more intensive mentoring program that reduced recidivism and made victims of all forms of violence, including many GSW patients, re-evaluate decisions and sometimes alter the paths of their lives.

To be clear, Batek is not opposed to guns. She is not looking to make a political statement or advocate for gun control. Quite the opposite. She was raised in a house where her father's gun hung on the wall in a holster. It was always loaded. Her dad was a hunter and taught his kids to shoot at an early age. Batek has guns in her own house. Her perspective is contrary to many at the hospital but comes from a place of experience. She is a proponent of the philosophy that "guns don't kill people, people kill people."

"But we have to figure out how to keep our kids safe," she said.

That pursuit started with a $150,000 grant to cover one caseworker for two years. Tyrone Ford became an SLCH mentor who responded to calls in the ER regarding gun injuries or other violence. All of the affected families were offered the opportunity to enter the study with a chance to have Ford work closely with the patient in the home or community. His approach involves motivational interviewing, which is a noncomfrontational form of counseling that has worked elsewhere with high-risk behaviors. However, Batek and Ford encountered multiple roadblocks. Even if a family agreed to participate, there was only a 50 percent chance they would work with Ford because half who agreed were randomly selected to be placed in a control group. That was mandatory for the study so that the long-term results from one group could be compared with the other.

Additionally, Batek knew that African-Americans, who make up the majority of violent gunshot cases, might be leery of the study. A history of unethical research has made many of them hesitant to participate in any kind of research. One such instance was the 1932 "Tuskegee Study," in which African-American men were told they were being treated for "bad blood." It actually was a study of men with syphilis. Participants were enticed with incentives and then misled and not given the proper treatment. The study lasted 40 years and ended with a class-action lawsuit. Studies have since highlighted the distrust African-Americans have for the medical community and the lack of interest in participating in clinical research.

After two years, Batek ended up with a control group and an intervention group with 35 patients each. She realized that the need to sign a consent form that outlined risks and liabilities along with the negative history hurt the chances of widespread participation. Hundreds of children and their families said "no thanks." But it was a starting point that was necessary if the program was going to expand.

Just getting to the point of launching the study was hard enough. Batek ran into roadblocks until Dr. Keller wrote a letter on her behalf supporting the proposal that had met with resistance despite the availability of funding.

"I needed someone to get through to the hospital administration," Batek said. "I didn't need it for the funders because they understand the social implications. It was the hospital I had to get on board. I went to Dr. Keller and said 'There are people who want to give money, but I have to have the hospital administration back it or they can't give it to me.' When I first started, I asked for $130,000, and the administration said it was too much to ask and to spend on the population we were working with. I knew I needed some support to get this through."

Batek received less pushback when she sought to expand after the initial trial. She received $450,000 to run the Victims of Violence Program for three years with two mentors — one male, one female. This time there was not a control group. The opportunity to participate was only restricted by an age range of 8 to 19. All families of patients who qualified could participate.

Interaction with social services begins almost immediately. The hospital is covered 24 hours a day by social workers. Among them is Bobbi Williams, who works strictly with trauma patients and their families. Her position was one of the additions made when SLCH received verification from the American College of Surgeons. One of SLCH's in-house chaplains also is available at all times, and families might use the Department of Psychiatry during the recovery process.

The primary goal of Batek's program is to serve as an advocate for the patient, regardless of the circumstances of the shooting. The truth is that no one can be sure what transpires in the early stages of a case, and Batek doesn't consider the details to be of consequence when services are being rendered.

Police officers often arrive in the ER with the intent of interviewing a patient who has been shot. The hospital has a longstanding relationship with St. Louis city detectives, but Batek found that road officers are frequently abrasive. In those cases, a social worker is apt to intervene before a conversation can get started.

"If they have no guardian, we see ourselves as their advocate," Batek said. "First and foremost, we tell officers that they are our patient first and then their suspect or witness."

A social worker interviews the patient when the time is appropriate. A guardian with knowledge of the details surrounding the shooting will be interviewed separately. This allows the stories to be compared for discrepancies, which are frequent, before the information is turned over to the police. If a parent has contact with their child before a social worker becomes involved, Batek knows the details provided by the child can be tainted. Often, adults distort or lie about a shooting if it occurred in the commission of a crime or if the firearm in question was obtained illegally or left unprotected in a home.

The circumstances surrounding a shooting often are murky and confusing. Batek recalled a young girl who arrived at the hospital a week after being injured. She was in dire need of treatment. But Batek knows there are reasons a patient might avoid the hospital if an injury seems minor. Some are intent on getting revenge. Some fear being targeted again. Once shooting victims seek medical care, their information is shared with law enforcement.

Mentors meet with victims and family members in their homes and communities. Whereas the initial Victims of Violence program allowed for a maximum of six meetings, the updated program requires a minimum of six meetings for a case to remain active. Patients are asked to develop goals. They range from completing school to getting along with mom or not roaming the streets. Success is measured by the ability to meet those goals. Patients have access to a mentor for one year. Batek, however, allows some flexibility because of the tight bonds that often develop and can lead to difficult separations. Mentors can advocate for children in their schools. They will accompany them to court if that scenario is involved. They tend to necessary services to assure the child's needs are being met. They learn about their lives and relationships and help guide decision-making.

"Often I find there's no responsible adult who's mentoring the child to serve as a role model," Ford said. "The child doesn't have access to any type of services at all. Poor economic status, gang affiliation, that kind of stuff. Just having someone there to motivate and bounce ideas off to provide a sense of care really helps them with their struggles and their stresses."

In the first three years of the program, SLCH treated 537 children who were injured in various acts of violence. Of that group, 443 were eligible for the program, and 113 decided to enter the mentoring process. Of those 537 violent acts, 213 were shootings with 40 accepting the free services. As of the start of the summer of 2017, none of the 40 original gunshot patients had returned with a subsequent gun injury. Zero percent recidivism.

The only patient in the program who returned with a gun wound in the first three years was initially a victim of an assault not involving a gun. However, of those who chose not to meet with a mentor, 58 returned with various injuries (17.6 percent). Out of that group, 18 originally were seen for gunshot wounds. Five of the nonparticipants subsequently died, four of them having been shot. Increased participation in the program had shown a clear and positive pattern in results.

"We can change the trajectory," Batek said. "I've been doing this long enough, and when I go to fatality reviews I see it go from assaults to stabbings to gunshots. It's a path. It's rare that a child who dies of violence has not been seen in our emergency department for minor interpersonal violence once or twice. If we end up getting them when they're physically assaulted and teach them coping skills, anger management and conflict resolution, you might not see them a year from now."

Those results were evident not only in a lack of repeat injuries but in other aspects of children's lives. In the case of one early participant, the initial changes were swift and promising. After completing all interventions, a male patient opted to move out of his grandmother's home to live with his mother because his grandmother was allowing him too much freedom in his choice of activities. In an email updating his progress, another social worker informed Batek that the boy was seeking more structure. His grades had jumped to As and Bs from mostly Ds and Fs the previous semester.

"I must say the young man has made major improvement," the email said. "I asked him why the change, and he replied that he was following the wrong crowd and he wants better for himself and that he was capable of doing better."

Batek is able to help some families with small financial contributions. She paid for a truck for one family to move out of a dangerous neighborhood, where it was feared a teen boy would get shot again. She helped one mother purchase beds for her children. When one child in the program talked of living in a home infested with bugs, Batek paid for an exterminator to spray to improve living conditions.

SLCH also arranged a summer outing available to all of the patients in the program. Batek and the mentors accompanied the group to a camp about 30 minutes outside of the city in the lush green hills of an adjoining county. There was some trepidation about mixing children from different city neighborhoods. But a day of team building and outdoor activities opened a door for children and teens to bond through shared experiences.

Some of those fixes are relatively easy. Getting all kids to end their risky behavior is virtually impossible. During the initial two-year study, one boy ended up being shot a second time. Charles was fortunate to have survived and needed to return only to have a bullet removed. He was 14 when he made that second trip to the hospital for a gun wound, coughing up blood. He contended that he and a cousin were minding their own business outside of a friend's house when the gunfire started without notice. His cousin was struck four times. Charles was able to leave the hospital the following day. The first time he was shot he was at a bus stop. He was hit in one foot and leg.

"I'm blessed," he said while waiting to have his bullet removed after the second incident. "They're telling me to stop doing the things I was doing. Stay to myself. Stop hanging on the street. I got shot again and that's telling me not to do that. It's just that I was hanging with the wrong crowd. I should have seen how things were going before I got shot."

Ford's job, in part, is to identify the actions that might have led to the violence. In many cases, he said victims are oblivious. They might be spending their time with people who put them in dangerous situations. An incident could be provoked by something as simple as a derogatory comment made weeks earlier. Ford had a pretty good grasp of Charles' background because he had known him for many years before the teen first showed up at the hospital.

"He has a hard time disassociating himself from those individuals. He doesn't want to be a square," Ford said. "He's a very smart kid who, when he's not affiliated with that environment, can get As and Bs without a sweat. But he does not want to be considered what they would call weak. It's been a hard four or five years for him.

"When I saw his name come across, I had to make sure we approached that one delicately, but he's one I think this program is ideal for if he would stay with it. With just a nudge in the right direction he could be a great kid. But it's hard for him to separate from that environment."

Ford begins his communication with patients by assessing their need to make changes and their willingness to do so. He evaluates community factors such as family, living conditions, school and friends. Typically, he finds that gun violence is the result of a conflict with a rival group, although not necessarily a gang.

Because many of the people he mentors were shot outside of their homes or in their neighborhoods, Ford knows to tread carefully. He has a broad knowledge of the St. Louis landscape and an understanding of the ease with which people can obtain guns in some areas. He has been trained to determine when a person is carrying and often can tell if he is approaching someone who has a weapon tucked in their waistband or on one of their ankles. He analyzes the way a person is walking. It might be with a heavy landing on one foot or with a limp. He might become suspicious if someone is wearing layers that can be used to conceal a gun.

"I know whether I need to go in protected," he said. "Most of the time I see kids in the evening. I'm not afraid by any means, but I'm not stupid either. By their address, I know what level of protection I need."

It is not unusual for Ford to find a disorganized home life and a student who is struggling in school. A mother might want to take steps to help her child but might not have the resources. In some situations,, Ford has to be creative. In one case he was dealing with a boy who not only enjoyed fighting but the outcome of having beaten someone. He redirected that energy to a boxing program sponsored by the police department and watched as the youth learned discipline and how to handle adversity.

When dealing with a GSW victim, Ford escalates the intensity of the conversation quickly because of the potential for more catastrophic injuries.

"I don't even go to death because I don't think kids are afraid of death," he said. "I go to paralysis or having to be fed through a tube or not being able to enjoy yourself like you want."

Measuring the success of the Victims of Violence Program is difficult. Batek believes that some people are alive today because of the work of the hospital's social services. SLCH has connected families with agencies that were able to help in various ways. Kids have received productive counseling. Perpetrators of the mistreatment of children have been jailed. Reduced recidivism indicates that children have altered behaviors that lead to shootings. Batek doesn't often see the long-term impact of the work done by her department. However, she has started to occasionally see people she helped long ago return to the hospital with children of their own.

"If they're living fairly productive lives, I feel we had a positive impact in the intervention we had," Batek said.

SLCH is a member of the National Network of Hospital-based Violence Intervention Programs, which grew to 34 members in 2018. Some of the programs were started by hospitals in the mid-1990s. Children's Hospital of Wisconsin in Milwaukee began Project Ujima in 1995. The hospital is possibly the only children's facility in the country that can rival SLCH's volume of gun trauma cases. Project Ujima claims a recidivism rate of less than 1 percent since 2004 among patients treated for various injuries.

But how do you put a price on success? Batek's program required more than $500,000 to operate in the first five years. The need to prove success will be a perpetual challenge if the program is to remain active.

"Will we change all of them? No," Batek said. "If it costs you $150,000 to hire a male and female social worker for a year and you change the lives of 10 kids, it's worth it. If we make a difference in the life of one kid, that's huge for me.

"If we can demonstrate that having a mentor with these kids can significantly change the direction of their lives, you would be hard-pressed to say you wouldn't spend $150,000 to do it. They spend way more money on diseases and ailments that don't impact society as a whole as much as violence does."

It took many years, but the program's positive impact on St. Louis youth was acknowledged with a significant expansion of services. As 2017 was coming to a close, funding was secured for the program to be replicated at Barnes-Jewish, Cardinal Glennon Children's and St. Louis University hospitals for patients 24 and younger.

The ER

The trauma bay can accommodate four patients if necessary — two on the main beds and two on foldouts. Emergency room personnel have practiced for moments when the room might be filled, or for something worse. Mass casualty preparation is a necessity at any hospital, and simulations of large-scale events are run at SLCH several times each year.

Fortunately, St. Louis has not experienced a catastrophe the likes of Columbine High School, Sandy Hook Elementary School or Marjory Stoneman Douglas High School. However, it doesn't take something of that scale to wreak havoc with the daily routine. In the event of multiple shootings, as happened one night in 2013 when 17 people were injured in St. Louis violence, the staff in the ER can be pushed to its limits. Of those 17, four from one shooting scene ended up at SLCH, although not simultaneously. Nevertheless, the repetitive arrivals of the injured that night created an overload at a time when the ER was busy, between 10 p.m. and midnight. One gunshot patient can occupy three physicians, four nurses, two medics and at least one surgeon. And that's just to get started. If multiple injured patients arrive at the same time, those awaiting treatment for illnesses, broken bones and other ailments are placed on hold.

"If we get one very sick trauma patient, it can almost shut down the system, especially at night with one attending surgeon," said Kim Quayle, the director of the division of pediatric emergency medicine at Washington University School of Medicine. "You can have half the nursing staff with that patient. It can shut down the flow of the emergency department. You have people leave without being seen, people being angry."

A GSW also requires an anesthesiologist, and a nurse from the operating room must make an appearance to monitor the possibility of surgery. A recording nurse documents the events as they unfold.

Planning for the manpower and organization that would be required for mass casualties falls under the responsibilities of Dr. Dee Hodge. The ER veteran was the obvious person for the task when it became known that early in his career he had planned a hospital evacuation during what became known as the Oakland Hills firestorm that killed 25 people in 1991 in California. Three years later, he was involved in care and problem solving after a 6.7 earthquake in Southern California. He organizes drills to cover various scenarios with the potential to produce an abundance of injuries. His hope, though, is that the plans never will be needed.

The hospital is required to hold two disaster drills each year to retain accreditation. Officials then document the process and create action plans based on the experiences. SLCH often does more than the minimum. Hodge oversaw a simulation of mass casualties from a plane crash on Interstate 70 near the St. Louis airport. The hospital has run earthquake drills and training for the handling of patients with the Ebola virus. In the wake of a tornado damaging St. John's Regional Medical Center in Joplin, Missouri, in 2011, SLCH simulated an evacuation in conjunction with other facilities, using dummies for patients. Lessons learned from actual events, such as the mass shooting in a theater in Aurora, Colorado, are incorporated. Unfortunately, there are enough incidents with extensive injuries from which to learn.

"This isn't just local and national, it's international. You learn from each one," Hodge said. "With Aurora, there was a lot of information to come out of that. Not only was the scene utter chaos, but it was late at night, so hospitals weren't well-staffed. There were patients brought in without advance warning. Police put patients in cars and drove. How do you handle all of that? The actual management of the injuries doesn't change. That's basic medicine. But how do you manage the system and numbers?"

A mass shooting is generally defined as an incident in which at least four people are shot during the same general time and at the same location. This does not include the shooter. Under those guidelines, the website massshootingtracker.org documented 1,939 mass shootings in the United States from 2013 through 2017. That covers 1,826 days. There were 38 shootings that involved four or more people in the St. Louis metropolitan area during that time. Fifteen of the 38 involved children or teens. One shooting was at the funeral for an 18-year-old. At least one was in a park where children were playing. Many involved crowds with children.

The organization Everytown for Gun Safety used FBI data and media reports to identify every mass shooting in the United States from 2009 through 2016. The organization tightened the guidelines by using incidents in which at least four people, not including the shooter, died. There were 156 mass shootings in those eight years. Children made up 25 percent of the deaths from those cases, which the group attributed to the significant number of domestic incidents.

If numerous gun trauma patients arrive simultaneously, SLCH employs a triage system that is relatively basic but requires quick analysis of injuries to get patients where they need to be based on severity. Those who arrive dead or with injuries deemed not survivable are tagged black. Critical patients are tagged red. SLCH can handle five critical patients at once. Patients who need medical attention that is not immediate are tagged yellow. Minor injuries sustained at the scene but not related to the event are tagged green.

The system is the same, regardless of the event that creates the injuries. And although gun deaths in Missouri have surpassed automobile deaths, according to the Violence Policy Center, and the rate of gun injuries remains high, SLCH has not run a simulation specific to a mass shooting or school shooting. These drills have been done elsewhere, including at the 2015 conference of the American College of Emergency Physicians.

"All of these situations have a lot in common, but they're also very different in a lot of ways," Hodge said. "In motor vehicle accidents, you may have a combination of head injuries and blunt force. Some need to go to the OR, some don't. With multiple gunshots, there's probably more chance of going to the OR."

* * *

If there is going to be shooting, it is best for everyone that it happen at a time when there is ample personnel to handle the case. But one of the problems that became apparent at SLCH over time was the presence of far too many people reporting to the ER for some GSWs. Numbers sometimes swelled in the trauma bay to the point that it was hard to know who was directly involved in the patient's care and who was just hoping for a role or there to watch. The crowd around the bed, which is dictated by specific tasks and positions, became a point of contention.

"People think they're helping, but they're really not," said Julie Leonard, who previously held Quayle's position. "It's a matter of learning to tune those people out."

The number of people available to work a case depends on the time of day. Staffing the emergency room for an average day is an undertaking that starts small and builds until full coverage in the afternoon and evening. Peak hours are from 3 p.m. until midnight when children and teens are most likely to be injured. The day's first shift starts at 7 a.m. with five nurses. Coverage increases later in the morning and throughout the day until 10 nurses are on duty. There could be as many as four attending physicians, who are trained in pediatric emergency medicine, working simultaneously along with two hospitalists, who are board-certified internists. At least two pediatric residents and one emergency resident are always available, with those numbers doubling during the busiest hours. Two pediatric emergency fellows work in the ER from 4 p.m. to midnight. For some, the arrival of a GSW means leaving a case that is in progress. For others, it's simply a matter of wanting to be involved.

The hospital eventually decided that crowds in the trauma bay had to be reduced to create a better setting for work to proceed as smoothly as possible. A time-consuming process of meetings and analysis was needed to determine the best and most efficient positioning of personnel in the room. The goal was to prevent trauma cases from becoming chaotic and to allow some people to focus on the regular flow of patients through the ER instead of being sidetracked unnecessarily.

When a gunshot victim arrives, every surgeon, physician and nurse who reports is given a specific assignment. Some of those assignments come with a position in relation to the bed. Those spots are illustrated on a diagram with stick figures on the rear wall of the trauma bay. After the process was thoroughly reviewed, the most critical positions remained the same. The team leader is stationed at the foot of the bed. There are spots for primary survey and airway duties. However, instead of having four physicians or nurses at the bedside, the analysis showed that two were sufficient. The new system required that each caregiver be given a sticker indicating a specific job. Those without a sticker are to remain behind a designated line in the room to reduce traffic.

"We're an academic center, so we're teaching," said Steve Brooks, the trauma department manager who oversaw the reorganization. "But sometimes there are too many people and you can't hear and can't think because there are too many opinions. What happens is that the pharmacy brings a friend they're training. Respiratory brings a friend they're training, and every subspecialty has a resident. They can't all be at the bed because no one can move."

The presence of family members of the patient can create further traffic. The ER allows two relatives to be present during treatment. Depending on the severity of the injury, emotions can run high. So, if there are more who want to be present, they are asked to rotate in and out of the trauma bay. If disruptive or deemed to be a threat, they are asked to leave.

"It's all about how you express grief," Quayle said. "One family may be very quiet and tearful, and another may be hitting walls and screaming. I had one family lay on the floor and scream."

One of Keller's roles is to teach. But the intensity of some cases does not allow for the time and patience needed for a resident to complete a basic chore. That dilemma became a balancing act when it came to determining who would be allowed to attend cases. Just when it appeared assignments were clarified and the number of bodies involved in a response reduced, Keller started to get calls. The director of the emergency room at Barnes-Jewish wanted to assure there would be room for residents who rotated into SLCH's emergency room.

"I said, 'OK, we'll tweak it so they get roles that benefit them,'" Keller said.

He was asked to make room for people in the ER fellowship at SLCH and various subspecialties until the requests trickled down to pediatric residents. Keller had to inform some departments that he was out of space.

"These are some of the sickest patients in the hospital," Keller said. "That's not where a trainee should be learning how to put in a chest tube. There are chest tubes that are needed in the OR or ICU on stable patients, and that's where they should learn. But when a patient's bleeding to death, I sometimes step up because I can't have a fellow doing it. But every time I thought I was done, someone said, 'My guys aren't getting enough airway experience.'"

Eventually, the staff reached a compromise whereby some trainees would have to wait on the sideline until the initial and secondary surveys on the patient were completed. By that point, some semblance of calm can be established and a course of treatment determined by the most experienced personnel.

* * *

Dr. Indi Trehan has worked sporadically in the ER during his tenure at the hospital. He's an emergency physician but has spent much of his time on research and working in Malawi and Laos to help children suffering from malnutrition. Nevertheless, he has seen at least 30 gun trauma cases during his ER shifts. Trehan's time in the small African country of Malawi has provided a different perspective on the mayhem and death he has witnessed from gun injuries.

One day he offered a blunt and seemingly emotionless description of a toddler who arrived with a GSW to the head. His words were jarring. But seeing children die is nothing new for Trehan, whose work in Malawi and other underdeveloped countries has placed him in the presence of horrific situations on a routine basis.

"There was one baby who was being held by his father, and there was some sort of drive-by," Trehan said. "The brain literally exploded all over the father. When he got here, there was some cerebral activity, but the skull was filleted open and there was brain goo everywhere. It was hopeless."

It's this type of reaction that has made co-workers suggest that Trehan has become emotionless. He concedes he is different from many he works alongside. Working continually with children who don't survive has, in Trehan's own words, made him "numb to death." It's not a matter of being uncaring, but the repetitive nature of his work has forced him to accept certain realities, whether he's treating gun wounds, malnutrition, Ebola or other contagious diseases.

"What I do most is research on malnutrition, and I've seen thousands of children die," he said. "The fact that this child is dying in front of me from a gunshot is no more meaningful to me than the fact a child is dying somewhere in the city where I don't see it. It's a tragedy in and of itself.

"If I see it, it's sort of more of a privilege because it reminds me to do something about it. It's a privilege to be part of that family's healing and comfort and be part of their lives at that time. All it does is make me want to keep doing the things I do, which is mostly research into public health problems. It motivates me to not just be a health-care provider in the ER. We need to be bigger than that. We need to speak out."

Trehan is an associate professor of pediatrics at Washington University and medical director at Lao Friends Hospital for Children in Luang Prabang, Laos. He previously spent about four months out of each year in Malawi with a research team that traveled throughout the country aiding children while looking for methods to keep more of them alive. The team grew to six nurses, five drivers and a business manager with a compound of homes and fleet of vehicles. Eight to 12 students worked at any given time.

From the capital of Blantyre, they trekked several hours to rural villages by vehicle over roads alternating from pavement to dirt and gravel. The team saw 3,000 children a year, knowing that 10 percent would die of malnutrition. The goal was to reduce that figure to 8 percent. Two teams traveled each day, leaving at 5 a.m. and returning in time for dinner. At each stop, enough food to last a few weeks was provided by Project Peanut Butter, an organization started by Washington University pediatrician Dr. Mark Manary. The team then returned to the villages to measure the results.

The battle Trehan fights in St. Louis almost seems to be the antithesis of the challenge faced on the other side of the world. When he works in Malawi, he sees children surrounded by people fighting to keep them alive, looking for ways to improve their chances. In St. Louis, he often comes in contact with children whose environment works against them, placing them in harm's way.

* * *

When Keller and Warner arrived at SLCH, the working relationship between the surgery department and ER was at a low point. Personality conflicts and bad attitudes among previous employees had led to poor communication. When there was communication, it was often not pleasant.

"I don't know if that contributed to a lack of progress, but there was animosity," Warner said. "People get territorial, and it's unprofessional. But if someone feels threatened by someone else rather than being calm and nice, they want to start screaming and yelling."

One case in particular magnified the divide between the two departments. It occurred early in Keller's tenure. The arrival of a severely injured patient prompted five attending surgeons to report to the trauma bay. When they arrived, they asked emergency room personnel to leave. It was viewed by many as a hostile takeover. The entire surgical staff had stormed the ER, planted its flag and claimed the territory as its own.

Many complaints followed, and Keller understood the anger. He was now working at a teaching institution, where part of his job is to train those in the ER as well as students how to handle trauma cases at a higher level. The working relationship had to improve. A new system was implemented to gather feedback on trauma cases after patients left the first floor to move upstairs. A medical student handed out surveys in the ER. The responses and comments were almost entirely negative.

"I didn't know who was in charge," one read. "He yelled at me," was a common complaint.

"It's a teaching hospital, and somebody is telling me to get out of the room. How am I supposed to learn and how to manage?"

One year of surveys was enough to shed a bright light on the problem. Not only did roles need to be better defined, egos had to be set aside. People had to learn to get along. Change started at the top with Warner and began to trickle through the ranks. Under previous leadership, the rift between personnel in surgery and the ER was said to be noticeable. Surgery seemed to disdain the ER leadership. Arguments would erupt in trauma committee meetings. The struggle for power was constant.

"The previous chief surgeon had a different interpersonal style and wasn't someone who engendered a lot of endearment," Quayle said. "It was night and day when Brad came, and that's a really important aspect of the service. Things can happen at bedside where you're not in agreement about how to provide care, which isn't ideal. Or it could be the larger picture. It's really that collaborative relationship that has to be at the bedside because it's so important in everything that we do.

"Brad came and made an effort to sit down at the leadership level. It's just very clear when someone wants to be accessible and available. When you call someone to ask a question, you get a clear sense when someone is being helpful and when they're being rude and not helpful."

Warner made the ER a place where everyone could, as Keller likes to say, "Play well in the sandbox."

A Matter Of Public Health

When social worker Risa Zwerling-Wrighton and 9-year-old Chelsea Harris were paired through a mentoring program, the arrangement was expected to last one year. Their paths crossed in an organization called Discovering Options, which was created to guide at-risk children away from drug use and other self-destructive behavior.

Zwerling-Wrighton quickly acquainted herself with many of Chelsea's closest relatives and sought to gain an understanding of the forces at work in the young girl's life. She helped Chelsea's great-grandmother gain custody. She aided the family in obtaining a low-interest mortgage. The one-year mentorship turned into two and then three. They remained close through Chelsea's teen years, and it became clear that college was in the future as she neared her 17th birthday.

Then Zwerling-Wrighton received a call on December 15, 2014, and two words turned her world upside down: "Chelsea's dead."

She had been gunned down in south St. Louis after exiting a car in front of a house she was visiting with a friend. She was struck twice while trying to run for the safety of the porch and died at a hospital. Her friend was shot multiple times and survived. Zwerling-Wrighton was distraught and overwhelmed by anger. She vented through writing, grasping for answers that weren't anywhere to be found. She had long con versations with her husband. The two decided to use her experience in social work and Mark Wrighton's position as chancellor at Washington University to pursue those answers. The Washington University gun initiative was born from a tragedy. Like the mentor relationship with Chelsea, its lifespan has been longer than expected. Zwerling-Wrighton helped shape the initiative during its infancy when the program was framed around public health. But first, Zwerling-Wrighton had to escape the initial emotions and the dream she concocted of a gun-free society.

"I realized that's not the role of the university. It's not what we could add to the dialogue," she said. "What we could do is look at the situation through a broad lens and understand how to implement change so there will be fewer deaths. We can do more research and figure out the best ways to intervene with children and gangs and teens and at-risk populations.

"The university has taken political stands but very rarely. They don't allow smoking on campus. Every once in a while they stand up for something. Mark and I talked about what was appropriate. Where are we most powerful? Then it was fairly simple to take a stand on gun violence. We don't have a legislative agenda. We are conveyors of information. We can do research, which is where we're powerful, and demonstrate what works, and policy follows from that."

Washington University's medical school sends many of its students and residents through St. Louis Children's Hospital for training and employs the hospital's physicians and surgeons. It was a natural pairing and stood to generate mutual benefits. Yet, it was a bold step because of the approach.

Public health is defined many ways. The American Public Health Association states it as such: "Public health promotes and protects the health of people and the communities where they live, learn, work and play. While a doctor treats people who are sick, those of us working in public health try to prevent people from getting sick or injured in the first place. We also promote wellness by encouraging healthy behaviors."

During its first year, the initiative was packed with seminars with an abundance of speakers and videos and panels, all of which led to a partnership with the United Way to form the St. Louis Area Violence Prevention Collaborative. And thus another grandiose vision was created. Organizers built a support system to reduce violent crime, recruiting the help of organizations that serve at-risk families and individuals.

From the start, the focus of the initiative — titled Gun Violence: A Public Health Crisis — was through a broad lens. Yet, organizers toiled for two years before addressing issues affecting children.

As the director of the university's Institute for Public Health, Dr. Bill Powderly recognized the power of focusing on children. The discussion of childhood gun injuries and deaths resonates with the public. He knew it would be hard to find people who didn't believe it was a problem worth tackling. Improving gun safety in the home could impact accidental and intentional shootings as well as attempts at self-injury. But even putting the spotlight on children and teens raises a dilemma inherent in most public health issues: the balance between an individual's rights and what's best for the community as a whole.

"For many strong supporters of the Second Amendment, there's a concern that some of the agenda with people talking about public health related to guns is a stealth attack on their rights," Powderly said. "They believe the only reason people are raising the public health issue is to take their guns. That is actually a false dichotomy.

"You can have responsible gun ownership. You can have controls that are completely within the bounds of the Second Amendment. It has regulation in it. When they framed it, I don't think they were talking about complete anarchy. You're looking at a number of facets that would be mitigated if there was a better culture of safety around the use of guns instead of taking guns away from people."

* * *

A study authored by Washington University researchers in 2016 showed that 75 percent of parents believe pediatricians should be allowed to discuss gun storage with their patients. Only 16.9 percent disagreed. The research was unveiled at a time when a law existed in Florida prohibiting doctors from having such conversations. The fallout from Florida and states where similar legislation was considered left many doctors unsure of their rights. Some were frightened to talk to patients about guns for fear of reprisal.

Michael Turmelle, who manages the hospitalists at SLCH, does not prohibit people in his department from having those conversations. Hospitalists are general pediatricians who provide care throughout the hospital in a variety of ways. Even during the height of the furor over Florida's gag order, which was overturned in 2017, Turmelle's division never had a discussion about policies regarding discussion of guns with patients. "I can't imagine someone telling me what I could discuss with patients," he said. "I'm not a politically active person by any means, but if that were to be something that came up in the legislature to limit our ability to talk to patients, I would become politically active. It would be something as a group I'm quite certain everyone in this division would be behind."

Missouri has a law regarding physicians, patients and guns. It stops short of prohibiting conversations. The law states that licensed health-care professionals in Missouri cannot be required to inquire as to whether a patient owns or has access to a firearm; document or maintain in a patient's medical records whether such patient owns or has access to a firearm; or notify any governmental entity of the identity of a patient based solely on the patient's status as an owner of, or the patient's access to, a firearm. The law goes on to state that it does not prohibit a physician from inquiring about gun ownership or access and documenting that information if "necessitated or medically indicated by the health-care professional's judgment."

Turmelle lives in the city of St. Louis, works there and sends his son to a city school. His experiences have fortified his beliefs. He has heard gunshots break the stillness of the night. His wife gets nervous being home alone. They do not and will not own a gun, although the issue often surfaces outside of his job.

He received a phone call one day at work to inform him of an incident at his son's school. An 8-year-old had arrived in the morning with a minor bullet injury to one of his legs. A teacher called for an ambulance. Later in the day, Turmelle was perusing a local news website and saw a photo of the child being wheeled out of the school on a stretcher. "That photo stuck in my head," he said. "You think of all these terrible shootings that occur, and this is a kid who's probably a year ahead of my son. Something happened in his life that he got shot and then went on his way to school like it's not a big deal."

The incident was one of many that made Turmelle think about the environment in which he places his child. What if this boy who had gone to school with a gun injury had been one of his son's friends? And what if his son played at that boy's house?

Dr. Fahd Ahmad, an ER physician who has dealt with many gunshot victims, joined a group of like-minded hospital employees to brainstorm about ways to educate families. His goal was to reach a point where he would have opportunities to talk to parents about gun safety or provide information through literature or videos when families arrive to have other ailments treated.

"To me, the ER is open game," he said. "There's no reason not to provide services that have nothing to do with your asthma attack. It's an opportunity to do a lot of things for a lot of families. If they're here for three hours for an asthma attack, and an hour and a half is nothing but sitting, we could be offering services. I'm not re-inventing the wheel, but guns are one thing we're not doing and very few, if any, places are doing."

Hospitalist Kathleen Berchelmann has never had qualms about raising the topic of guns. Several times a year during her tenure at SLCH, she met with a patient or family that had been involved in a gun incident, typically a suicide threat that fell short of a tragic ending.

"When you have a teen holding a gun to their head in the home, you need to have no guns in that home," she said. "Parents never agree to it. I've never had a parent agree to remove guns from their home. They tell you they're locking the guns and all the steps they're taking to secure their guns. They say they'll think about it, but never do they say, 'Yeah, they're gone.'"

Multiple studies have shown that access to guns, whether in the home or elsewhere, increases the possibility of suicide. One such study from 2014 by researchers from University of California, San Francisco, compiled results from 15 investigations, showing that a person with access to a firearm is three times more likely to commit suicide. In Missouri, there were 202 documented suicides with a firearm among children 17 and younger from 2000 to 2016, according to the Missouri child fatality review program. Gun suicides increased significantly in the years 2013 to 2016, when the number was 69 percent higher than the previous four-year period. The deadliest years since the annual report started in 2000 have been 2016 with 20 and 2014 with 17.

David Hemenway is a professor of health policy at Harvard School of Public Health and wrote a book called "Private Guns Public Health." Writing about the risks and benefits of a gun in the home, he cited a study of self-inflicted gun wounds that included 30 suicide attempts that were unsuccessful. More than half of the 30 said that their suicidal thoughts had lasted for less than 24 hours. Two years later, none had attempted suicide a second time.

Berchelmann spent a brief amount of time with such families before they moved through the system. She saw all of the possible responses from those who are feared to be suicidal: anger, frustration from a lack of success, joy from a lack of success or denial of the attempt. When a gun is used in a suicide attempt, the rate of death is 85 to 90 percent. With that in mind, Berchelmann was just happy to have a chance to talk to these kids. As an added defense against suicide, ER social workers at SLCH began in 2017 to tell families with children who were seen because of suicidal thoughts about the prevalence of firearms used in suicides. If open to the discussion, the families are offered gun locks.

The Washington University study showed that 13 percent of respondents went to a pediatrician who raised the topic of gun ownership or storage. One-quarter of respondents said a firearm was stored and loaded in their homes. The research concluded that "avoiding direct questioning about firearm ownership and extending the discussion about why and how to ensure safe storage of firearms to all parents may be an effective strategy to decrease firearm-related injuries and fatalities in children."

Nevertheless, SLCH decided on a more direct approach. Families now are asked on admissions paperwork if there are guns in the home, if they are stored in a locked container, if bullets are stored in a separate locked container, if the guns are unloaded and if they have trigger locks.

* * *

When Keller stepped to the podium to speak about children and gun injuries in March 2017, Washington University had been operating its initiative for two years. The emphasis was mostly on gun violence — intentional acts of assault, homicide and suicide. He was addressing a room filled with generally like-minded thinkers.

Keller made the point to his audience that the focus on gun violence was too restrictive based on the data. He had been saying as much for a while. When Keller and his colleagues completed their five-year study of gunshot trauma cases at SLCH, the results told Keller that the strict emphasis on intentional and violent shootings was missing a large part of the story. The report that was first presented in Chicago had plenty of information regarding intentional acts of violence with guns. But the surprising number of accidental injuries prompted the removal of "violence" from the title of the paper when it was finalized and published in The Journal of Trauma and Acute Care Surgery.

With close to one-third of the GSWs among patients 16

and younger being classified as accidental, Keller concluded that solutions needed to be tailored to address disparate issues. Determination of accidental injuries was made through patient reports and interviews with hospital social workers.

"We felt gun violence was a misnomer," he said. "I've been saying that since the onset of this program. It's not just violent mechanisms. It is a significant impact on child health. It has a strike rate as high as anything we see. All communities are affected in my mind. No one is exempt who shouldn't care about this."

Over a five-year span from April 2008 to March 2013, the hospital treated gun victims from 94 ZIP codes in Missouri and Illinois, covering the city, suburban and rural settings. SLCH's coverage area reaches as far as 250 miles. Incidents determined to be accidents involved handguns, pellet guns, shotguns and rifles.

Keller's presentation was timely. In preceding weeks, two shootings involving siblings occurred in the city of St. Louis. In the first, a 12-year old boy was shot in the head and died after he and his 9-year-old brother were left home alone and found a gun in their house. In the other, a 6-year-old girl was shot and killed by a sibling. Charges were filed against the adults living in the homes in both cases. Not long after, a 4-year-old in St. Louis unintentionally shot himself in the hand and mouth with a parent present in the house. A 2-year-old got his hands on a gun and shot and killed his father while he was sleeping. A 13-year-old accidentally shot his brother, who was 10.

In February 2013, Keller and Drs. David Jaffe and Bo Kennedy went public with their belief that gun injuries and deaths among children should be classified as a public health crisis. An article they authored was published and generated a considerable amount of negative comments, including a letter penned by

Dr. Stephen Lefrak, also at Washington University School of Medicine. He wrote in part, "When social problems are medicalized, then the solutions are looked for in medicine and biology. This is an extremely dangerous tack as we learned during the eugenics movement in the United States and during the years of National Socialist Germany." Undeterred, Keller persevered with his position.

"In the future, we need to separate intentional and accidental shootings and deal with these as two different aspects," Keller told his audience. "Clearly some action should be directed to safety initiatives."

* * *

Public health initiatives have existed for decades, even centuries. Attempts to curtail diseases or deal with issues of polluted water started with ancient civilizations. During modern times, massive efforts began during the cholera outbreak in the 1840s when Dr. Thomas Latta developed the intravenous saline drip, which helped save many lives.

"That was the time when regulations started to follow from evidence and science," Powderly said. "Much current policy started in the mid- to late-1800s around infectious diseases as more science came out. We have, in the course of developing public health policy, had this debate about individuals' rights to do whatever they want vs. the impingement of that freedom on the health of the rest of the community, where the acts of individuals are potentially dangerous. We almost always come down on the side of community health."

In more than two decades working at SLCH, Dr. David Jaffe embraced that idea. Jaffe arrived at SLCH in 1991 to help create the Division of Pediatric Emergency Medicine. The staff included only a handful of employees, and he became the division's first director. His earliest training came in Philadelphia at a time when education specifically focused on pediatric emergency medicine didn't exist. However, he agreed during those years to participate in a newly designed, advanced program with one other trainee. They eventually laid claim to being the first fellowship-trained pediatric emergency physicians in the country.

During his tenure at SLCH, Jaffe saw enough GSWs to conclude that the problem clearly fell into the public health realm. His study of other issues reinforced the idea that a reduction in shootings, injuries and deaths could be made if there was a push to make the type of changes that occurred with the automobile, tobacco and lead industries.

"Some people have made those fighting words," Jaffe said. "But when we've had the appropriate research and the kind of information the scientific community can bring, we've made significant changes in this country."

However, restrictions have long been placed on gun research. In 1997, Congress passed a bill that effectively barred the Centers for Disease Control and Prevention from doing any studies that could be viewed as promoting gun control. Funding to the CDC was cut by $2.6 million, which was the amount spent by the organization the previous year on gun research. Larger amounts were retained for research on diseases that affect a smaller number of people than those impacted by guns.

After the mass shooting at Sandy Hook Elementary School in Newtown, Connecticut, President Barack Obama reversed the ban on CDC research. However, the

U.S. House of Representatives Appropriations Committee denied an attempt to fund research by the CDC. Adding to the lack of new information was a decision by the National Institutes of Health to allow funding to lapse on firearm research projects. The constraints are an ongoing frustration for those trying to reduce shootings and improve care.

"It really makes you have to be creative in terms of funding for how you're going to do these projects," Dr. Brad Warner said. "High quality requires a lot of resources for statistical review and database development, and the design of a database requires a significant effort with people who need to be educated. The research of today is the practice of tomorrow. Slowing research or halting it keeps us from moving forward. It keeps us from saving lives, curing disease and treating people better than how we do today."

Jaffe believed that the slash in funding kept the CDC from producing complete or accurate statistics on gun injuries. The hands-off approach is the polar opposite of the battle that was waged to improve auto safety and decrease deaths on America's roads. It started with the enactment of the National Traffic and Motor Vehicle Safety Act in 1966 as a path to improving the safety of automobiles. Then came seat belts, shoulder straps, airbags and a long list of other regulations. That effort produced significant results. Traffic deaths peaked in the early 1970s and have been decreasing since. Although gun deaths also have declined, the number of gun deaths and traffic deaths from 2013 to 2016 was virtually identical, according to the CDC.

Jaffe spent considerable time during his final years at SLCH voicing his concerns about childhood gun injuries and deaths. As president of the Academic Pediatric Association, he helped formulate written testimony to the Senate Committee on the Judiciary to present ideas about how to reduce gun violence while respecting the Second Amendment. The paper highlighted the lack of data due to restrictions on research. That remained a frustration for Jaffe, forcing him to accept that any change would come at a snail's pace.

"Even though we haven't banned cigarettes, we've significantly regulated the environment for the good of public health," he said. "Is that going to happen in the next five years with guns? No. It's not something the government is going to regulate in my lifetime. Maybe not anyone's lifetime."

His tenure as president of the APA came as there was a significant amount of attention on mass shootings. Jaffe used his platform to write multiple articles about the issue. A lover of music, in particular singing, he found ways to combine that passion with his pursuit of gun safety. Jaffe was a member of the Gateway Men's Chorus in St. Louis and couldn't resist using music and music theory as a backdrop for his writings.

To start one piece, he referenced the song "How Can I Keep From Singing" with the lyrical content adopted by folk musician Pete Seeger, who helped the song become something of a social activism anthem. Jaffe quoted lyrics to open an article that came in the wake of the Newtown mass murder:

> *"Thro' all the tumult and the*
> *strife I hear the music ringing;*
> *It finds an echo in my soul —*
> *How can I keep from singing?"*

Jaffe proceeded to call for a ban on assault-style weapons and large ammunition magazines and pleaded for more support for mental health services and an end to restrictions on firearm research. It was an example of the freedom of expression he and others are allowed without repercussions as university faculty.

In his farewell address as the outgoing APA president, he spoke almost exclusively about firearm injuries and deaths among children. In doing so, Jaffe framed his talk as a "symphony in four movements" and used the concepts of rhythm, dissonance, polyphony and harmony to structure his discussion.

Jaffe was considered a quirky character at SLCH, maddening to some in the hospital. But he longed for something that could be perceived as progress in the battle to reduce the shootings. In the end, he was just another voice seeming to holler into a great void.

* * *

The Washington University gun initiative started with a dozen people sitting around a table at the Ritz-Carlton. The high-end hotel is in Clayton, where the median household income is more than $95,000, and the median home costs $642,000. This is not a focal point of problems in the St. Louis metropolitan area.

"Some of the criticism is that we're in an ivory tower," Zwerling-Wrighton said after that meeting. "What do we know? We don't get it. That type of thing comes from students who work in the community and sometimes feel embarrassed to say they're Wash U students. But we're getting out of that tower."

That was her pledge in the days and weeks after the initiative was organized and publicized. It would take until January 2017 for Chelsea's shooter to be sentenced to life in prison after being found guilty on charges of second-degree murder, armed criminal action and assault. In the meantime, university Chancellor Mark Wrighton did not merely give his blessing to the university's initiative; he seemed to embrace the enterprise as an important piece of the school's mission.

As the chancellor spoke to graduates at the 2016 commencement ceremony, he addressed the problem not only as a national and local issue but publicly recognized that it could strike close to campus. That in itself was a bold step as the leader of an institution of higher learning ranked among the most prestigious in the country. It's a university that recruits some of the top high school students from around the country and the world.

As he acknowledged the class that graduated 50 years earlier, Wrighton noted in his speech that the first cigarette warning labels had debuted in 1966. That was one of the tipping points in the public health battle against big tobacco.

"But other public health problems from at least 50 years ago are still with us," he said. "It was in 1966 that sniper Charles Whitman killed 13 people and injured another 31 from atop a tower at the University of Texas. Today, death and injury from guns represent one of our country's greatest public health challenges, with about 30,000 deaths annually and about double that number of injuries annually from guns.

"Roughly two-thirds of the deaths are suicides, and others are homicides and accidents. One month ago, just a few hundred yards from where I am speaking, an assailant in a passing car on Forsyth Boulevard discharged a gun multiple times, aiming at a member of our community. Fortunately, in this instance, the victim will recover and no bystanders were injured or killed.

"Over a year ago, our university undertook an initiative to reduce death and injury from guns, addressing the problem as a public health challenge. It is my hope that those returning for their reunion 50 years from now will view this public health crisis as one dealt with long, long ago."

As the university's initiative unfolded, it spread to the community and the classroom, giving rise to new efforts. Classes were added to the curriculum to expand upon the effort. One course was designed to help students with the preparation, analysis and presentation of data, using a gun violence archive and St. Louis crime data. Another addressed gun violence as a public health issue. Professors and speakers addressed the history of firearm access and legislation, violence-intervention programs and how physicians treat and educate patients in the wake of gun injuries. Students in the class created proposals to integrate the topic of gun violence into the medical school's curriculum.

The university also sponsored a project in which students developed entrepreneurial concepts targeting a reduction in gun violence with monetary awards to help the most promising ideas move forward. The winning students received $1,000 to advance a plan for secure gun storage by partnering with entertainment venues. Other students received $750 to help form an organization led by youth who are impacted by gun violence to create further initiatives to reduce shootings. The initiative led to the creation of the Guns, Suicide and Safety Workgroup, which explores ways to reduce the suicide rate in Missouri. The effort quickly generated participation of service organizations, police, politicians and gun shop owners.

Missouri Representative Stacey Newman, whose district includes Washington University, was inspired to create the Children's Firearm Safety Alliance (CFSA). Newman's launch into the world of politics in 2000 resulted from her daughter, then 6 years old, writing a letter to entertainer Rosie O'Donnell to express her opinions about guns in homes. Her daughter appeared on O'Donnell's TV show. After being elected, Newman quickly became known throughout Missouri for her stances on gun issues. Through the CFSA, she hopes to reduce the number of unintentional deaths through education as well as legislation that will place more responsibility on gun owners for the safety of their firearms.

However, she faces an uphill battle as a Democrat in a Republican-controlled state. Her most recent attempt came in the form of a bill introduced in December 2017 to create specific circumstances that would constitute endangering the welfare of a child. Included was a section regarding the securing of a firearm in the presence of someone younger than 17 or in a home where someone younger than 17 is living. As of fall 2018 the bill had two readings but a hearing had not been scheduled. Previous attempts to pass similar legislation in Missouri have failed.

* * *

Unfortunately, the trend that developed in the midst of the gun initiative only served to make the job more difficult. Michael Brown was shot in Ferguson in August 2014. Chelsea was killed in December of that year. The initiative began the following spring. SLCH had seen a decrease in GSWs over a couple of years, but that was about to change.

After the number of cases dropped to 37 in 2013, the hospital treated 58 in 2014, 78 in 2015, 84 in 2016 and 73 in 2017. The Ferguson incident marked the beginning of an uptick as the hospital treated 254 patients with gun wounds from August 9, 2014 — the day of Brown's death — to the end of 2017. Also disturbing was a trend toward younger victims at SLCH. The average age from 2008 to 2013 was 14.2 years. From 2014 to 2016, the average age dropped to 13.2 years, with 31 percent being pre-teens. The rate of accidents remained high at 31.3 percent for all ages seen at the hospital during those three years.

Ten years after Keller started at SLCH, the landscape had changed dramatically. Conflicts involving law enforcement led to increased shootings between police and citizens. Incidents of shootings involving children, even toddlers, were on the rise. Rolling gun battles between passengers in vehicles on streets and highways were more numerous.

After the number of shooting victims treated at the hospital declined from 2010 to 2013, they increased by more than 100 percent within two years and were still on the rise as 2017 came to an end.

Aftermath

When he thinks about his first 11 years at St. Louis Children's Hospital, Keller has a clear image of the improvements made in the treatment of gunshot wounds. Those years also have worn on him mentally, maybe even physically, because of the regular arrivals of kids who have been shot. The surgical staff has again dwindled, forcing more of the responsibility back onto Keller and Dillon. But despite the fatigue, Keller can take pride in what he has helped to create.

"We are really slick in taking care of these patients," he said. "We are able to handle the worst of the worst because of things we have in place. If you get to the hospital with vital signs, you're going to survive. That wasn't necessarily the case before. "Some would still rather take a different direction in what we do, but there's no movement to do it. Am I burning out from it? Yeah. Do I want to get up at 1 a.m. for the next 15 years to do this? No."

The repetitive nature of treating GSWs has dramatically improved the system. Resuscitations are more successful because blood products are given to patients early in the process rather than IV fluids and blood components. The introduction of a mass transfusion protocol has allowed some to survive who might have previously died. The skills of everyone involved have been upgraded or fine-tuned. The hospital has an anesthesiologist on site around the clock whereas previously one might have had to respond from home. The hospital has improved its review process, allowing deficiencies that might have been over-looked in the past to be identified. There are few GSW cases that are overwhelming because everyone involved is better trained and more comfortable with the process.

There is still plenty that frustrates Keller. One thing stands out. The only thing he has seen emerge from the horror of the Sandy Hook shootings is a "Stop the Bleed" campaign implemented by the American College of Surgeons.

"There's been no impact in preventing the bleeding," Keller said. "Let's deal with the gun problem. There's no one in government who will do anything. It's an absolute embarrassment."

The doctors, nurses and students who comprise the staff of SLCH will come and go in years to come, just as they always have. New players will be initiated in the dance of treating gun trauma. Many will reach the same conclusions as Dr. Keller, fighting the same battles years after he is gone. Washington University's gun initiative may fade, or ebb in its influence, perhaps to be replaced by a different effort under different leadership. But for those who were pierced by bullets as children, for those whose bodies were repaired at SLCH, or for those whose loved ones could not be saved by the hospital — the trauma of gun violence and accidents endures.

* * *

Sara is the girl who, at age 6, had her midsection destroyed by a shotgun fired by her brother. When she returned to the hospital to have the colostomy bag removed, her tiny body seemed too fragile to have survived such a violent intrusion. Sitting in her hospital bed, she wanted to watch a Barbie movie and asked for a doll to keep her company. She hadn't eaten for four days.

"Can we get one more thing from the gift shop?" she asked her mother, Dawn.

Sara handled life with the colostomy bag better than expected. She took care of its maintenance at home and at school. She traveled with Dawn and her father, who is a truck driver, to Florida for a vacation. On the beach, she wore a swimsuit that covered the bag as if it didn't exist. That was Sara's approach after months of carrying Daisy — her nickname for the bag — everywhere she went.

The guns were removed from the house the night of the shooting. The 12-gauge shotgun was a family heirloom that Dawn hoped would be returned. The 20-gauge that produced the injuries was of no interest. "They can melt that into a paper-weight for all I care," she said.

Dawn felt life was regaining some semblance of normalcy. She had taken parenting classes and seen a therapist. Her boys had been to a therapist as well. She was still married. After receiving a bill for $200,000, some friends at Dollar General held a fundraiser to help with expenses. Eventually, that bill was eliminated mainly by Medicaid. The incident did not change Dawn's opinion of guns.

"There are times when they are a necessity just for protection," she said. "If I had it to do over again, it would be more along the lines of changing the way I deal with the boys than the way I deal with the guns because if he had listened, not only to me but the fact his father told him not to touch them, I don't think there would have been an issue."

* * *

Byron is the mother of Maurice, the young man who returned to SLCH to have a bullet removed from his buttocks. But the procedure did not close the book on gun violence in her family. Before the incident, she had seen problems escalating in her neighborhood for some time. The family lived in what was then District 8 in the police department's breakdown of the city. It was, at the time, the city's smallest district with Kingshighway as its western border, thus providing a direct route to SLCH.

Two months before Maurice was shot, Byron's 18-year-old niece was involved in an incident that left her with non-life-threatening gun injuries. A friend in East St. Louis had recently found her 10-year-old son after he was struck and killed by a bullet as he was sleeping in his bed. Maurice's injury and the mayhem in the neighborhoods of District 8 were causing significant problems for Byron's young daughters as well. She sent them to live with their father in St. Louis County to escape the violence and the constant fear.

She had wanted to move for some time but didn't have the means to do so. She was looking for a job the summer Maurice was shot. Their house had been damaged by a fire, forcing them to move. Now, she was living in a neighborhood with older people where she felt more secure around folks who presumably knew how to work out their issues without resorting to weapons.

"My baby girl was so terrified that she would sleep in the tub where there are no windows," Byron said. "They've got to have some type of stability where they don't have to get up every morning and hear about someone being shot. They've seen a lot. One guy got killed in his van across the street. My baby got up one morning they were shooting, and she grabbed her pillow and slept in the tub. If something falls, she jumps and gets in the tub. When kids need counseling for something like that, I think 'She can't stay here.' Since she's been out in the county, it's working. She's at peace. She said she doesn't have to sleep in the tub no more."

* * *

Marcus Johnson Sr. sat with his back to a window that overlooked his front yard in north St. Louis. He's the man who lost his 5-year-old son to a shooting after leaving a park outing with his family. As he gazed out the open front door, the neighborhood was quiet. Each time a car passed, Marcus turned to look out the door. He would take a long gaze, make sure all was well and then return to the conversation.

Four months had passed since his son was killed. The calls from the police had slowed. The status of the case was unclear. Marcus and Quiana, who was pregnant, considered moving after the name of their street was published in an article about the shooting. At that point, their comfort level diminished considerably, as did that of their children.

"I got to make sure nobody hurts my family," he said. "That's the stress we got to wake up and live with every day. All of this stress, every day. We don't know if this dude is going to pull up and start doing to our house like he did to our car. That's my main stress. I don't want to be sitting on the porch, talking to my wife, and the guy pulls up and boom, boom, boom, boom."

As of the summer of 2015, Marcus and Quiana had 10 children between them. She brought four into the relationship, and Marcus had three. They had three together, and another was on the way. They have lost two. One boy died as an infant, suffocating in his sleep. After Marcus died, the others wanted to get out of the neighborhood.

"They don't want to be in the house anymore," Marcus said.

When school ended in spring 2015, they weren't. Quiana's oldest son went to stay with her sister and her oldest daughter with her mother. Marcus' children were dispersed between his father and an aunt. The family had been torn apart by the loss of a little boy who endured more pain than most in his six short years.

The focus in the Johnson home became raising the children and keeping them from harm's way or from finding other trouble. Marcus Sr. had his own problems as a youth. He was born in a car traveling between Memphis and St. Louis at the Arkansas-Missouri border. He landed in prison for a short time before meeting Quiana, who he credits with changing his life. He has scolded his kids for wearing their pants slung too low or for placing questionable photos on social media sites. He is worried for children in his neighborhood, especially the ones who approached him one day with five handguns tucked into their waistbands, looking to make a trade.

Marcus was on disability in the months after Marcus Jr. died and had a lot of time on his hands. He and Quiana spent most of their time around the house. He tried to do odd jobs here and there, but there was too much time to think about what had happened. They hoped a day would come when all of the shooters would be caught so that they could have a party creating some closure. In the meantime, Marcus continued to receive offers from people wanting to settle the issue of little Marcus' death.

"I've got homies ready to go out and kill somebody," he said. "It could be an innocent person. I don't know who done this. I want to know, but I don't. I ain't going to go out and shoot up the whole street, so I let the law handle it."

Marcus can't stop the gun violence any more than all of the doctors can, or the nurses, social workers and academics.

Even the best hospital can't turn the tide. It can only seek to rescue those who get washed ashore and alert others to the danger.

But Marcus knows he holds a key to stopping the cycle of gun violence – at least for himself. He knows he needs to fight any vengeful impulses, if nothing else than for the children.

"God blessed me with these kids, and I've tried to turn my life around. I don't want to do that because I'm going to lose everything."

Thank You

Special thanks: St. Louis Press Club, Jackie Ferman, Abby Wuellner, Katrina Frazier, Mo Schmid, Dick Weiss, Judy Martin Finch, St. Louis Publishers Association, and the St. Louis Post-Dispatch.

About The Author

Stu Durando has written on sports for the St. Louis Post- Dispatch and Las Vegas Sun for three decades. He is from Los Angeles and has lived in St. Louis for 21 years.

Made in the USA
Lexington, KY
22 December 2018